Waiting Tables

FOR VERY GOOD MONEY

a guide for ambitious waiters and waitresses

Waiting Tables

FOR VERY GOOD MONEY

a guide for ambitious waiters and waitresses

Richard Montauk
and
Adam Murray

AUTHOR BIOGRAPHIES

Richard Montauk

Waiting Tables for Very Good Money is an outgrowth of Richard's forthcoming book, *How to Make Real Money During College,* which profiles some 140 well-paid jobs available to college students while they remain full-time students. Richard's early experience in the restaurant industry was varied and extensive, including work as a busser during college, consulting to an international beverage and hospitality company while working for the corporate strategy consulting firm, Bain & Co., and later helping run a busy social club in Belgium that employed numerous wait staff and bartenders.

Richard's primary occupation since 1991 has been as a consultant to college and graduate school applicants applying to the world's leading universities. He is also the author of numerous books regarding college and graduate school (Law and MBA) admissions. Richard has degrees from Brown University, Harvard University, and Stanford Law School.

Adam Murray

Adam is a graduate of the University of California at Berkeley, where he double-majored in English and American Studies. He has been working in restaurants since his community college days before transferring to Berkeley, with jobs ranging from cashier, bartender, and beverage director to server. He now works as a manager at Zazie, one of San Francisco's leading restaurants, which is noted for its excellent treatment of its employees, including waiters. (For a detailed look at his career before he started work at Zazie, see his resume on page 77.)

TABLE OF CONTENTS

INTRODUCTION

Waiting tables is one of the oddest jobs in America—not because serving food to other people is peculiar, but because most of the 2,500,000 people in the profession basically stumbled into it. Very few waiters thought long and hard about whether waiting tables was the right job for them. Instead, their thoughts probably ran along these lines:

- I need to make some money right now.

- I don't have any particular skill that's in great demand.

- I hate the idea of a desk job.

- Lots of my friends have worked as waiters, so why don't I give it a try?

- The restaurant down the block needs servers, so I guess I'll apply for a job there.

In other words, there usually was no carefully thought-out strategy to their choice of work. This book takes a very different approach. We think waiting tables offers not only a very good opportunity to make a substantial amount of money but also to have a really enjoyable time in the process. However, we caution you that you are unlikely to prosper if you are lazy: waiting tables well requires hard work. *You need to be proactive to do a good job—and to get a good job.*

This is not meant to frighten you. In fact, we'll guide you through every step of the process. In the chapters ahead:

- We'll teach you everything you need to know about the industry, even the lingo used in the business

- We'll show you how and where to get the best jobs

- We'll walk you through each step of the application process—from putting together online applications, cover letters, and resumes, to mastering the various types of interviews you'll encounter

- We'll show you the basics you'll need to master as a novice server and then show you what you need to learn to become a true professional

- We'll teach you the ways in which you, as a true professional, can maximize your income by getting the best shifts and best stations, developing regular customers, getting good tips from foreigners, and more

- We'll show you how to move up to the management ranks, if you choose

- We'll show you how to change restaurants, including getting jobs at the fanciest of fine dining restaurants

- And so much more.

You might think that this is a lot to accomplish in only 252 pages. And we agree: it is a lot. In the chapters that follow, we've concentrated on what matters most. In the process, we skipped some of the most technical matters that you can and should pick up on the job. For example, this book won't show you how to fold a napkin 94 different ways or the nuances of "Russian" service, or how to pronounce the names of French wines. Little of that is likely to be useful in any given restaurant, and if you have mastered what we cover, your restaurant will probably be happy to teach you the additional fine points of what they require.

Who Should Read This Book?

This book is designed to help anyone waiting tables make the most money possible. It will obviously be useful to those just starting out as a server. But we think it will be equally valuable to those already in the business, including those who have been waiting tables for years. The only exceptions: Servers who have already mastered what's in this book and are presumably already making several thousand dollars a week.

How Much Impact Can This Book Have On Your Income?

Waiters at better restaurants earn much more than those at other restaurants. In fact, waiters at some of the restaurants we included in our research earn more than ten times as much as the waiters at various of the other restaurants. The range of average earnings per shift at the various restaurants we surveyed was from less than $50 to more than $500.

Getting hired at the best possible establishment is only half the battle. The best servers in a restaurant typically earn much more than the lesser servers earn. This is true not just at fancy, expensive restaurants, but at much less pricey ones, too. For example, at the Sidebar at Whiskey Row, a Louisville restaurant that specializes in hamburgers (with an average price of $16 with fries—albeit with fancy cocktails on offer), the best servers make $55 per hour, triple or quadruple what some of the other servers make.

The implications are obvious. Getting a job at the right restaurant, and then becoming one of the top servers there, can increase your earnings dramatically.

AN OVERVIEW OF THE RESTAURANT INDUSTRY

The restaurant industry is a large and important part of the American economy. It employs 14 million people—ten percent of the country's workforce. One-third of Americans had their first job in a restaurant, and nearly half of all adults have worked in the industry at some point in their lives. Although many chose to leave the industry (or at least to change employers—the industry has a very high turnover rate), others moved up. Approximately 80 percent of restaurant owners started as hourly employees, as did 90% of managers and chefs.

The Importance of Restaurant Service

Excellent service is the easiest way for a restaurant to distinguish itself and develop repeat customers who are happy to bring their friends. Poor service, on the other hand, can easily destroy a restaurant. Insiders report that approximately 70 percent of the complaints about restaurants have to do with service, with food quality, décor, prices, noise, and parking making up the other 30 percent. As a result, owners and managers are constantly on the lookout for the types of servers who will be assets for their business.

Why People Work as Waiters and Waitresses

It's not surprising that so many people are attracted to jobs waiting tables. These jobs offer a number of benefits:

- The satisfaction of pleasing people, many of whom are stressed, exhausted, or in need of entertainment when they arrive

- Meeting interesting people

- Getting free meals as well as an opportunity to sample a wide range of food and drink

- A flexible schedule

- Good pay (in some but not all restaurants)

- A steppingstone to management or ownership

On the other hand, serving jobs have a number of potential disadvantages:

- They can be physically demanding and emotionally draining

- Many restaurants pay poorly

- Some people are pulled into an alcohol (or drug) culture among the staff

Of course, many people work as servers simply because they need money. In any event, given that more than 2.5 million people work waiting tables in the U.S., we are not going to discuss whether someone should or should not work in the field. Instead, we assume that many people will do so—and can benefit from our advice about how to get the most out of their work.

INSPIRATION FOR THE BOOK

Co-author Richard Montauk was writing *How to Make Real Money During College,* which discusses some 140 jobs that college students can get for above-average pay. For each job, he intended to provide resources readers could access for helpful information—books, magazines, websites, blogs, and soon. The one job that he could not provide useful additional resources for was waiting tables, despite the frequency with which college students work as servers. He then contacted Adam Murray, whom he knew to be an experienced (if young) waiter with an interest in writing, to start work on this book.

OUR RESEARCH

In writing this book, we conducted traditional research of the field—books, articles, blogs and the like regarding the restaurant industry, waiting tables specifically, and even looked to apply relevant articles from sources such as the *Journal of Applied Psychology*. But our most important learning, in addition to insights from personal experience, was from our hundreds of interviews of people in the industry.

The majority of our interviews were with owners or managers of restaurants, but we also talked to more than five dozen servers, as well as caterers, banquet captains, consultants who train servers, restaurant and hospitality investors, lawyers who specialize in representing restaurants, and others. (For detailed information about those we interviewed, see the Acknowledgments at the end of the book.)

Those we interviewed work at restaurants and other establishments that cover a remarkable range. They are located in more than thirty states, in large cities, suburbs, and small cities and towns. With entrée prices ranging from less than $10 to more than $100, some are very unpretentious, some are "regular," and some are fancy indeed. A rough breakdown of the types of restaurant would include:

Airport	Green
Barbecue	Grill
Bistro	Hotel
Brasserie	Local, resort, tourist
Burger	Locavore
Café	Organic
Caterer	Pizzeria
Chain, corporate	Pub
Country/private club	Seafood
Delicatessen	Steak/chop house
Diner	Vegan, vegetarian
Ethnic (see below)	Wine bar
Family, independent	Winery

In addition to interviewing people at a full range of "American" restaurants, from Cajun to Hawaiian, deli to Tex-Mex, and New England to Southern, we interviewed personnel at multiple restaurants of each of the following (self-described) nationalities:

Asian	Korean
Brazilian	Lebanese
British	Mediterranean
Central American	Mexican
Chinese	Persian
Cuban	Peruvian
Ethiopian	Portuguese
French	Puerto Rican
German	Russian
Greek	Spanish
Indian	Thai
Irish	Turkish
Italian	Vietnamese
Japanese	

We also interviewed key people at dozens of other restaurants. In short, we have been as thorough as possible in gathering the information that underpins this book.

Understanding the Industry

Chapter One

What Restaurants Seek In a Server

The Ideal Server

The ideal waiter or waitress may not exist in reality, but would probably have the following characteristics if he or she did:

Attractive; neat and clean appearance. Customers want to interact with someone who is attractive, and definitely want to have their food handled by a neat and clean person.

Friendly, enthusiastic, happy. Your mood affects the mood of both your colleagues and diners, so a warm and upbeat person is highly desirable.

Desire to please other people. Successful servers reap a great deal of satisfaction in making other people happy. Yes, they may want to make as much money as possible, but they are genuinely pleased that they can do so by bringing a smile to the faces of those they serve.

Intuitive understanding of people's desires. A good server quickly understands whether a guest wants a great deal of interaction or to be left alone. She knows if her customers want menu suggestions or to make their own choices based solely on the menu write-ups, and so on.

Energetic. Waiting tables often involves long hours on your feet doing very physical work. Being able to do so without flagging, and without losing your cool, requires substantial energy.

Team Worker. Waiting tables in many restaurants requires a team approach. Someone who fails to get on well with others will face problems in these establishments.

Good communicator. Restaurant work requires constant communication—with the kitchen, other servers, bussers, the host, and of course, your guests. For example, to be an effective sales person rather than simple order-taker requires you to inspire guests to order more—or more expensive—items. Note, too, that good communication skills are associated with intelligence, preparation, and knowledge—and thus have an impact upon how you and your restaurant are viewed.

Good memory. The best servers have to remember a lot, including how each menu item is prepared, which wine and other drinks best complement the food, food and beverage orders, preferences of regular patrons, and local history and points of interest.

Patience. A server's job seems designed to test one's patience because you are dependent upon other people (hostess, servers, bussers, cooks) to perform your job, and your customers are often fussy and short-tempered.

Able to handle stress. Servers experience physically and emotionally stressful circumstances on a regular basis. The physical stress includes being on your feet for many hours, rushing back and forth, and carrying heavy trays. The emotional stress may involve difficult customers, too many tables to cover if a fellow waiter fails to show up, or a kitchen falling behind and making diners mad.

Flexible and responsive. Servers have to be able to "expect the unexpected." Some shifts will be busy and others painfully slow. One moment you may be waiting on a table full of kids celebrating a birthday; the next, a group of octogenarians with hearing or other aids. And your personal after-work plans may need to be abandoned when a large group shows up just before the kitchen closes.

Polite. Servers who are not unfailingly polite—with guests and with co-workers—upset people needlessly.

Fit with ambiance of the restaurant. Tattoos and ripped fishnet stockings can be an asset at a trendy spot in the East Village of Manhattan, while being able to speak Italian and mingle with a sophisticated clientele would be valued at a very upscale Italian restaurant.

Reliable. The restaurant business in general is volatile: all the tables can be empty at 7 pm and jammed at 7:30 pm; a large take-out order may get canceled at the last minute, and so on. But for the most part, the least reliable element in the business is the staff. Many servers and other personnel arrive late or not at all, or simply quit without a moment's notice. As a result, restaurant managers value reliability highly. They want servers who do what they say they will do—above all else.

Charisma. In some restaurants, but not all, charisma is valued. Servers who are able to project their personalities to good effect are generally valued in restaurants where diners hope to be entertained as well as fed.

Physical coordination. It goes without saying that a clumsy waiter means plates dropped, other servers crashed into, and other disasters.

THE REAL WORLD

Managers do not expect to find the perfect employee—with all the traits listed above—but they hope to find servers with as many of these characteristics as possible. Different restaurants prioritize different characteristics. A hip restaurant in a heavily-touristed area posted the following ad just before this book was published.

WE NEED YOU!

We're looking for full-time waiting staff—especially people who can also cross-train as hosts and bartenders.

You must have an amazing personality, a genuinely friendly attitude, and a can-do nature. You need to believe in always delivering an exceptional experience for every one of our guests. We want them to feel like they are a guest in your home.

Most of all, you must be reliable and fit in with our existing team.

If you want to work with like-minded people who are friendly, positive, and love working in an exciting restaurant, then we want to hear from you. So, if you're interested in being part of a team that people love, pop in and let us know why we should hire you.

This restaurant is clearly looking for team-oriented, upbeat servers—thereby prioritizing personality and attitude over prior experience and professional skills. A very fancy, high end restaurant serving a traditional French cuisine might look for a very different profile. It would value those with substantial professional experience in a comparable environment and, because it wanted waiters to provide unobtrusive service, would avoid hiring dramatic, look-at-me servers. Thus, a big personality would be a plus at the first restaurant and a minus at the second.

Virtually all restaurants hope to find loyal, highly motivated employees who are willing to work odd hours. And given the frequent turnover in the industry, servers who will stay for an extended period are especially valued.

RESTAURANT MANAGERS DISCUSS
WHAT MAKES A GREAT SERVER

"The best waiters are passionate about this industry. They enjoy going out to eat, appreciate good service/food/cocktails/ atmosphere—and want to create that experience at their own restaurant."
Corporate casual restaurant manager

"Pleasing the customer is the most important thing in the business. If servers don't understand that, they have little hope."
Fast casual restaurants' owner

"The best servers love what they are doing."
Seafood restaurant manager

"The best servers can be relied on to do their best even when no one is watching."
Steak house manager

"The best servers pay attention to their customers; they don't just take orders."
French restaurant manager

"The best waiters need minimal direction. They also keep themselves busy—or ask their manager what they can most usefully do."
Casual restaurant owner

"The best servers are able to multi-task. They can look at five tables in different stages of their meals, handle each one, and do so while talking pleasantly with them rather than being robotic."
Irish restaurant manager

"The best servers treat the restaurant like it's their home and they're letting a guest in. Mediocre servers see it as step one: do this, step two: do that; etc.—it's just a job for them."
Hotel restaurant manager

"They have to enjoy people. There are lots of folks who claim they're people persons, but they're not."
Corporate casual restaurant manager

"The best are self-sufficient, problem solvers, and improvisers."
Upscale hotel restaurant manager

Under-Performing Servers

Restaurant owners and managers often feel overwhelmed by under-performing servers who, for instance:

- Seldom wash their uniforms
- Reek of cigarette smoke
- Expect praise, pats on the back, and gold stars just for showing up

- Fail to help fellow servers who are in the weeds
- Are unwilling to accept suggestions (let alone orders) to improve their performance—because they already know everything
- Won't put their cell phone down
- Can't or won't concentrate on the job
- Show up late or not at all

We have all encountered a server like this. Let's call him Chris. Chris is slow, scatter-brained, and eager to get off the clock the moment he gets on. He loses track of checks and cash, fails to bring guests the beverages they ordered, and mixes up the orders of different tables. Chris makes so many mistakes that other servers can't possibly cover for him. They need to protect and privilege their own tables above everything else. When Chris jeopardizes his fellow servers' time and tables, they will inevitably start filing complaints against him with management.

OWNERS AND MANAGERS DISCUSS THEIR HIRING CRITERIA

GENERAL PERSPECTIVE: UPSCALE RESTAURANTS

"We want people who are super-willing to learn. We hold intensive training every week. Our servers are expected to be a combination of sommelier and after-dinner cheese expert."

Wine bar manager

"The fine dining experience has changed so much: people don't come just to dine, they come to be entertained. So we look for someone who can entertain our guests."

Fine dining restaurant owner

"The turnover problem is so great that restaurants (including ours) will lower their standards if they think they'll be able to keep a server for an extended period."

French restaurant manager

"We look for communications skills and a passion to engage with diners. (Talking with people is a lost art. We have trouble finding people under the age of 25 who do so.)"

Fine dining chain president

"Composure is the most underrated thing when it comes to working in the industry."

Restaurant consultant and former server

"We want someone who is flexible and willing to learn."

Fine dining restaurant owner

GENERAL PERSPECTIVE: OTHER EMPLOYERS

"For catering, we look for older, more professional waiters."
Restaurant and catering business owner

"We want people who are intelligent, optimistic, and display leadership and communication skills."
Latin restaurant manager

"We're a pooled house. I want to find people who can work together as a team."
Corporate casual restaurant manager

"We want people with an "excellence reflex"—who do something as well as possible because it's the right thing to do."
Latin restaurant manager

"We hire for character, and train for skill."
Latin restaurant manager

"Willingness to work and reliability are critical. I hate to train someone for two weeks and then have him quit."
Asian restaurant owner

"We hope someone has had longevity in a prior job."
Casual restaurant owner

"We want people who are willing to work during our slow season as well as our busy season."
Corporate casual restaurant manager

THE IMPORTANCE OF PERSONALITY AND ATTITUDE

"We hire on the basis of attitude, personality, and willingness to work. People skills. It's relatively easy to teach the mechanics of service."
Italian restaurant manager

"You can teach everything except personality."
Casual restaurant owner

"I look for personality—I can teach the skill and knowledge, but not the personality."
Corporate casual chain manager

"Personality can overcome lack of experience and knowledge—but only if the person has energy and is willing to work."
Latin restaurant manager

"Serving skills can certainly be learned, but the right attitude toward service is essential—it has to be positive and passionate."
Mediterranean restaurant manager

"Performance is determined by attitude—how well you can be managed and take direction."
Steak house manager

"No experience is necessary. You just need a bubbly attitude, an ability to work with people, and a willingness to work and to learn."
Seafood chain restaurant manager

"Attitude and personality are the most important factors. I can train almost anyone to do the job."
French restaurant manager

THE IMPORTANCE OF FIT

"A lot of what makes a good server is the ft with the clientele and work culture here."

Fine dining restaurant manager

"Someone who is generally serious would be a great pick for a five star hotel, but not great at a chill dive bar. A goofy, high energy person would be the other way around."

Restaurant consultant and former server

KEY HIRING CRITERIA

Attitude versus Experience

When we started researching this book, we made the assumption that the best and possibly only way to get a good or great serving job was to acquire experience at less demanding, not-at-all fancy restaurants, and then move up to a somewhat better restaurant after you established yourself as a fine server. You could then repeat this exercise several times. If you played your cards right over a number of years, you could eventually get a high-paying job at a busy, pricey restaurant.

We were wrong—or, at least, we were partly wrong. Some restaurants do indeed require that would-be servers have prior experience. This is most common among fancier, pricier restaurants, for two reasons. Their customers are more demanding and these restaurants can be choosier about whom they hire, because serving jobs at them are desirable. However, even among upscale restaurants, many care little about experience and a great deal about attitude (willingness to work hard, learn a lot, and take direction) and personality. Most instructive in this regard were our conversations with a slew of managers of upscale steak houses. At some, substantial experience—and experience of the right sort (i.e., in fine dining restaurants)—was an absolute requirement. To others, the right attitude, personality, manners, and grooming mattered a lot and experience little or not at all. At restaurants with less choice of servers, experience was less often required. And even when it was, the experience might not need to have been serving experience. Any restaurant work, such as bussing or hosting, might suffice.

The implications of this are profound for would-be servers: experience has value, but may not limit your ability to get very well-paid serving jobs.

The Value of Experience

Experience still gives applicants an edge. At a minimum, it shows that someone knows what to expect of a job waiting tables. It can also show someone's commitment to the industry. And of course it may mean that someone has developed highly relevant knowledge and skills, which will reduce or eliminate the need for additional training.

But even though experience is valuable, it will generally not make up for a poor attitude or personality. Multiple owners and managers made it clear that they would not hire someone with a questionable attitude no matter how good their prior experience.

So even if your experience is relatively limited—or even nonexistent—you can still aim for a job at an upscale restaurant. If you can show that you love being a waiter, ache to do your job extremely well, and have a pleasing personality that you project by engaging easily with customers, you stand to get jobs well above your skill and experience level.

Relevant Experience

Restaurants tend to value experience most highly when it's relevant to the position they are looking to fill. For example, ten years of experience working the cash register in a McDonald's isn't particularly valuable if you want to work as a waiter (or even a cashier) at a high-end restaurant.

In a service-oriented business like the restaurant business, however, even experience acquired in non-restaurant settings can be relevant and extremely valuable:

- Retail jobs that involve customer interactions.
- Jobs that involve handling customer complaints or providing customer service.
- Jobs that show you to be sociable and an easy conversationalist.
- Jobs that require projecting your personality or entertaining people. For example, working children's parties as a clown or character performer.

- Jobs that require lots of attention to detail.
- Physically-demanding jobs with long hours.

Also, a record of showing up on time without missing a day has value, as does remaining at the same employer for an extended period. Dependability is particularly prized in the restaurant business because it is not very common.

OWNERS AND MANAGERS DISCUSS THE VALUE OF EXPERIENCE

WHERE EXPERIENCED IS REQUIRED

"We typically require one to two years of serving experience, but when we're desperate for servers, we'll take someone with no experience."

Asian restaurant manager

"We require 3-5 years of fine dining experience."

Steak house manager

"We like people to have enough experience—usually six months or so—to have learned the basics, including how to react to customers, and how to handle diffcult situations and guests."

Corporate casual restaurant manager

"To work dinner shifts, you need to have had a year or so of experience in a nice restaurant, either upscale casual or fine dining. Without experience, you start with breakfast and lunch shifts. You can develop wine and menu knowledge as you do."

Hotel (upscale casual) restaurant manager

WHERE EXPERIENCE IS NOT REQUIRED

"We prefer people who have experience, but personality trumps experience."

Irish restaurant manager

"We prefer that servers have no serving experience because they're easier to train."

Upscale restaurant manager

"You don't have to have experience. We can teach you what you need to know."

Steak house manager

"Sometimes it's better if you don't have any experience because it's easier to teach habits than break habits."

Casual restaurant chain manager

"A common problem with experienced waiters is that they're set in their ways and don't want to do things the way we require."

Mediterranean restaurant manager

TYPE OF EXPERIENCE REQUIRED

"You need fine dining experience in a restaurant we respect. The duration is not that critical, but multiple short stays in a number of places would be an issue."

Wine bar manager

"We require at least six months of restaurant work, but not necessarily as a server."

French casual restaurant manager

"You need to have worked in a restaurant at least as a busser, runner, or bar back."

Hotel restaurant manager

"We require some experience, but not a lot. The experience could be gained at any sort of restaurant."

Mediterranean restaurant manager

"We request five years of fine dining experience, but we would make an exception for someone who had directly comparable experience of even as little as a year, such as in another great steak house."

Steak house manager

"A person needs some hospitality experience, even if it's not as a server."

Steak house manager

HOW CANDIDATES WITHOUT EXPERIENCE START

"Without experience, you start as a host. Once you've mastered that job, you are made a server."

Corporate casual restaurant

"Without experience, you'll start as a busser. You'll learn how to greet people, serve water, clean the table, and take orders. You'll also learn the menu well over three months."

Asian restaurant manager

"You need basic skills, such as where to place the cutlery for appetizers and where for main dishes. Otherwise you'll start in the back—washing up, prepping, and plating."

International Asian restaurant manager

"With no experience, we start someone as a server's assistant. To be hired as a server, one year of serving experience is necessary."

Asian restaurant manager

"We start an inexperienced person as a host, to get her feel for what is expected."

Fine dining restaurant owner

THE EXPERIENCE VERSUS PERSONALITY
AND ATTITUDE TRADE-OFF

"They don't need to have much experience if they have the right personality."

Fine dining restaurant owner

"Experience helps, but it isn't the end-all. You can't train speech patterns, appearance, personality, intellect, for example."

Steak house manager

"We hire on the basis of attitude, personality, and willingness to work. It's relatively easy to teach the mechanics of service."

Upscale Italian restaurant manager

"The amount of experience we require depends upon the person's demeanor."

Seafood restaurant manager

"You don't really need the best work experience to be hired. If you are engaging, make good eye contact, come dressed appropriately, and ask good questions, you're likely to be hired."

Fine dining restaurant manager

"If someone has the right attitude and personality, we'll start them as a runner or food server's assistant while they develop their wine knowledge (as well as learning what service involves)."

Steak house manager

"I can hire someone who has a good attitude—cares about people, enjoys being part of their celebrations. I can train that person to do whatever is necessary to serve. If I hire someone who knows how to serve, I can't train her to have the right attitude."

Casual restaurant chain manager

"Experience can be a bonus, but we hire people with little or no experience when they have the right attitude."

International upscale restaurant manager

DIFFERENT PERSPECTIVES ON EXPERIENCE

"Rarely does experience ever make or break my decision to hire someone. Some of the best servers I've ever worked with only had a year of experience, and I've worked with awful workers that have been in the industry for ten-plus years."

Restaurant consultant and former server

The Value of Relevant Knowledge

Some establishments, particularly the most upscale ones, are less concerned about a server's knowledge of serving techniques than about her knowledge of food, wine, beer, or liquor. Wine bars, for example, generally require that all of their servers know a substantial amount about the wines they offer. Unlike some fine dining restaurants, they do not have a wine specialist, or *sommelier,* on staff, so the servers are expected to help guests select wines. In addition, the food serving required of wine bar servers is relatively modest relative to what might be required in a fine dining restaurant. As a result, many wine bars would be much more likely to hire someone knowledgeable about wine without serving experience, than an experienced server who lacked wine knowledge. Proprietors of these wine bars have found that it is easier to teach serving techniques than wine knowledge. (At fine dining restaurants both experience serving and knowledge of wine may be required.)

A WINE BAR MANAGER DISCUSSES REQUIRED WINE KNOWLEDGE

"You need a good knowledge of wine. It doesn't have to be Spanish wine knowledge; it could be French or Italian, for example. If you know French wines, you'll be able to learn Spanish wines. You'll need that to serve customers, of course, but also to be credible with your colleagues. We simply wouldn't hire someone who knew little about wine."

Spanish wine bar manager

Information for College Students

College students make up a large percentage of wait staff in America. Given their need for part-time jobs with flexible schedules, this is hardly surprising. The benefits of working as a waiter, from a student's perspective, include:

- Flexible hours

- Potentially great pay for a limited number of hours of work

- Free or discounted meals (and often opportunities to take food home, too)

- Work that does not follow them home or interfere with their studies

- A network of friends and contacts outside of school

- As an added bonus, many college students find that working to pay their way through school elicits substantial diner sympathy, which can translate into extra-large tips.

Some restaurants are particularly suited to college students, including those where:

- Waiters are allowed to swap shifts, giving student servers the flexibility they need to accommodate their own shifting schedules. (Bear in mind that it's still a good idea to request time off for finals months in advance.)

- You are not expected to go drinking with other servers at the end of the evening.

AVAILABILITY AND OTHER CONCERNS

Restaurant managers often worry about how often, and how regularly, college students will be able to work. Most expect you to work multiple shifts each week. It's usually best to be conservative in what you commit to initially. If you claim that you can work four shifts a week, but then find that you are falling behind in your classes because you are working too much, you will have to maneuver to reduce your workload. You may end up annoying your manager early in your tenure at the restaurant, or even being fired.

Some students delight in having their friends visit them at their restaurant, but this can lead to problems at restaurants, especially those that are not college hangouts. Your friends are likely to:

- Expect free food and drink

- Distract you from doing your job

- Upset other diners by not fitting into the restaurant's normal ambiance (if it is not a college hangout)

TAKING ADVANTAGE OF SERVER OPPORTUNITIES AT YOUR SCHOOL

Many colleges, even small ones, have a faculty club that serves meals to faculty, administrators, and college guests. These clubs usually hire students for server, busser, and other positions.

Many universities also have catering operations to service the many events they host. They usually favor hiring their own students. Other schools have strong ties with one or two local catering firms. Although these firms may not have such a strong incentive to hire local students, they often do so in order to cultivate goodwill with the schools.

Colleges also offer opportunities to develop relevant knowledge and skills:

- Culinary arts courses

- Language courses

- Study abroad programs (why not in a fancy wine-producing region, such as Bordeaux or Piedmont, where you could learn the wines and cuisine as well as the language?)

- Bartending courses (presumably not for credit, of course)

- Many college career services host "etiquette dinners" as a means to prepare students for job interviews conducted over a meal. You can use them as a means to develop a better understanding of the table settings and service appropriate to a more or less formal meal

SUMMER JOBS

Many college students take advantage of their summers off by working for restaurants in hotels and resorts, whose need for servers and other personnel peaks during June, July, and August. For instance, in New England, the restaurants of Cape Cod, Nantucket, Newport, and numerous other locations operate at full tilt during the summer. With free-spending visitors on vacation, servers can make a great deal during the summer—more than they might make in a typical office internship.

Since many of these restaurants depend upon college students to fill a large number of positions during the summer months, relatively few can afford to require their applicants to have a great deal of experience. Thus, even a small amount of serving experience (even in an unimpressive restaurant), or just hosting or bussing experience, may be enough to land a good job. So, too, may a good attitude— energetic, willing to work hard, and hoping to learn—without any experience suffice to get you hired.

What's most likely to be required, however, is being able to show up at the start of the summer season or soon thereafter. If your college does not finish its spring term until mid-June, for instance, you may be unable to land a summer serving job.

You can improve your chances of getting a good summer serving job by:

- Working in a restaurant during the school year or prior summer in any capacity, so that you know (and can communicate in an interview) the basics of restaurant work.

- Visiting the resort in advance of the summer season to interview with local restaurants, rather than waiting until you have finished the school year. (Spring break is generally an ideal time to visit.)

Waiting until the season is in full swing can cost you a server job, leaving you with less attractive and less lucrative options, such as a job hosting or bussing.

- Making it clear that you are not a delicate snowflake—you can readily accept criticism and won't fold if you get yelled at.

- Dressing the part. The most desirable restaurants to work at in heavily-touristed areas serve an up-market clientele, so dressing appropriately for this clientele is important.

- Recognizing that seasonal restaurants often handle a very high volume of customers. This means that high energy and efficiency are essential for servers, bussers, and other staff.

- Recognizing that some seasonal restaurants permit time off (working five shifts a week) and others do not (working seven shifts a week). If you interview with a restaurant in the latter category, you will fail to impress if you admit you are looking forward to a fun-filled, easy summer.

- Being very clear about when you can start work. Even better, show the lease you have signed (with the starting date indicated). Then keep in close touch with the restaurant until you start, reaffirming that you will be arriving as planned.

The seasonal nature of resort restaurant work is obvious: it peaks in the summer (or winter, in the case of ski resorts). The same is true of many restaurants in college areas. Since many college towns are filled with students September through May, and relatively empty during the summer, restaurants may be happy to hire servers for the academic year and let them go during the summer. Thus, a college student on a standard September through May academic calendar may be able to work through the academic year at a nearby restaurant and at a resort restaurant during the summer.

At some other college-area restaurants, the reverse is true. With so many student servers leaving during the summer—whether because they have graduated or taken jobs or internships elsewhere—these restaurants are desperate for summer servers. This offers an excellent opportunity to get a job during the summer at a short-staffed restaurant and then keep the job during the boom period when school is back in session.

Jobs During the Academic Year

Many restaurants in college towns, or college areas of cities, staff up for the increased business they expect as students return in August or September. The key to getting the best serving jobs is not just to have the right attitude and (perhaps) the right experience. Nothing substitutes for being one of the first credible applicants. So consider returning to college a few weeks early to get first crack at the best serving jobs.

SEASONAL RESTAURANT MANAGERS DISCUSS HIRING COLLEGE STUDENTS

"We open May 1, but we start hiring at the beginning of March."

Corporate casual restaurant

"It's helpful to research the town and the restaurants you want to work for. Come here before the season starts. Approach us during a quiet time, such as when we open (11:30 am) on a Monday or Tuesday."

Upscale independent casual restaurant

"We serve an up-market clientele, even though we're not a tablecloth, fine-dining restaurant. If you show up for an interview in a T-shirt and jeans, you're signaling that you want a job at any restaurant that will hire you. You aren't targeting us specifically."

Upscale casual restaurant

"I prefer to hire athletes because they only need to be shown something once or twice to learn it. I also like that they expect to work hard and as part of a team. Plus I know that if I yell at them they won't internalize it and worry; they'll just try to improve."

Corporate casual restaurant

"You don't need to have worked in a restaurant before, but it's important that you have some work experience. I don't like to see candidates who've never worked before."

Corporate casual restaurant

"We call references. Period."

Upscale independent restaurant and corporate casual restaurant

APPENDIX: HIGH SCHOOL STUDENTS

Many high school students work during the school year, whether informally cutting a neighbor's grass or more formally in a retail shop. If you decide to work then, you will presumably take into account many factors, from location to hours, nature of the job to pay scale. Restaurant work may or may not be an obvious choice. Your first job in a restaurant might not pay any more than a typical retail job, for instance, and may require much more effort. On the other hand, that retail job may not lead to more lucrative employment a few years later. (Retail is a notoriously low-paying sector.) Restaurant work, however, can become substantially more lucrative as you move up from host or busser to server (and even more so if you become a bartender). Thus, working in a restaurant might prove to be an investment in your future as much as a job for today.

To move up as quickly as possible in the restaurant world—to become a server, and a very well-paid one at that—learn as much as possible in your first position(s) and demonstrate the right attitude and work ethic. You may well be promoted at your first restaurant. But if you want to change restaurants, perhaps because you are going away to college or just because you want to work in a fancier (and higher-paying) restaurant, an excellent recommendation from one of your managers will help you do so.

The ideal reference will attest to your great attitude and work ethic, including your:

- Showing up every day, on or ahead of time

- Working hard throughout each shift

- Being a team player, with a willingness to do whatever helps the staff, even if it was not part of your stated job responsibilities

- Learning as much as possible about how to perform your job

- Learning other jobs such as bussing, food running, even washing dishes—whether by helping out, cross-training, or filling in

As the rest of this book highlights, the payoff to getting a good serving job and then making the most of it can be extraordinarily high. You can lay the foundation for this during high school.

CHILD LABOR LAWS

Child labor laws limit the hours and jobs teen-agers (under the age of 18) can work. In California, for instance, minors 14 to 15 years of age are allowed to work up to 3 hours on a school day and 8 hours on a non-school day, and between 7 am and 7 pm when school is in session (or until 9 pm during the summer). Sixteen and seventeen year olds are given somewhat more freedom. They are legally able to work up to 4 hours on school days and between 5 am and 10 pm (and 12:30 am before non-school days).

The types of jobs minors are permitted to perform is also limited in many states. This often rules out performing dangerous agricultural and manufacturing jobs, but may also preclude any restaurant jobs that involve handling alcohol. Thus, in some places minors cannot work as servers or even bussers or food runners in restaurants that serve alcohol. In others, they cannot work in any capacity in restaurants that serve alcohol.

Some states require that both parents and their minor children sign agreements specifying the minor's hours and duties.

Types of Restaurant

There are a wide variety of restaurants and other establishments that serve food, such as bars, country clubs, and so on. This section cannot do justice to the full range of such places, but it does at least sketch the landscape any job seeker will confront.

The restaurant industry classifies restaurants in very broad categories:

- *Fine dining* restaurants are full-service restaurants that emphasize high quality food, décor, and service. Most offer a wide variety of wine, beer, and spirits.

- *Casual dining* restaurants include a wide range of establishments. Many serve moderately-priced food in a casual atmosphere. They often have a full bar with separate bar staff and may be part of a restaurant chain. There are two prominent sub-categories of casual dining which differ in important ways from the standard casual dining restaurant. *Family style* restaurants may offer food on platters for diners to help themselves. Aiming to attract families with small children, they serve no alcohol. *Upscale-casual* restaurants feature a relaxed dining atmosphere with relatively pricier food.

- *Fast food* restaurants—often termed *Quick Service Restaurants* (QSR)—focus on speed of service and include everything from local food carts to industry giants such as KFC and Burger King. Diners order food at a front counter or kiosk, then carry the food to a table. When the meal is finished, the diner disposes of the waste in a trash can. Many QSRs offer drive-through or takeout service. Pizza QSR s usually offer delivery. Although these restaurants have a large staff, they do not employ servers. A sub-category of fast food restaurants is *fast casual*. These are primarily chain restaurants that prepare more food on site than a conventional QSR (which largely prepares the food at a central depot). Food quality and prices are somewhat higher at fast casual restaurants than at a typical QSR.

A Closer Look at Restaurant Types

We feel the industry's own categorizations of restaurants are too broad to be of much use to us, so what follows is a somewhat different categorization of various establishments, along with a look at how attractive each type is for servers.

Fine dining restaurants

These are generally the best places to work, based on the ratio of pay to work. The bills are high and the customers are expected to tip well. They may offer full benefits, profit sharing, and 401K plans with employer matching of contributions. As a result of the pay, benefits, and working conditions, there typically is very little turnover. Wait staff positions at many of these restaurants are coveted, giving the restaurants their choice of servers. Some high-end restaurants expect waiters to be career servers and most look for waiters with substantial relevant experience.

Waiters have small sections; they are expected to take extra care of guests. And they are expected to know the food, liquor, and wine menus thoroughly.

Some fine dining restaurants take a traditional approach to service: unobtrusive, quiet, sophisticated. Others now prefer a more engaging, charismatic style of service. In the former, expect to be ignored by customers and treated more or less as a servant. In the latter, you will more likely be regarded as an individual human being.

Caution. Bear in mind that some fine-dining restaurants may look like highly desirable places to work because they are expensive, but fail to turn their tables because their guests tend to eat late and then linger for the remainder of the evening. If you are unable to get some guests to come early and request your section (see page 243), you may not make a great deal of money. Twelve guests paying $75 each may generate only $180 in tips (at a tipping percentage of 20%). You would be better off at a restaurant with average bills of $50 per head, serving 30 people in the course of an evening, since that translates into $300 or so in tips.

THE NEW STYLE OF HIGH-END SERVICE

It used to be that the ideal service in high-end restaurants was invisible but always hovering. A waiter would never introduce himself to the table or let even a drop of his personality show through. Professionalism was equated with invisibility—being always available without intruding, let alone being personal.

The ideal is in the process of shifting. Some high-end restaurants still prefer what might be called the European or continental impersonal and invisible style, but others have moved toward a more American approach. These restaurants assume that diners like a very personal touch, with waiters being recognized as professionals consulting with the diners rather than being mere servants to them. More and more restaurants therefore are now selecting waiters in part for their personality, looking for those who will charm and engage diners. Extroverted charm is thereby often prioritized over technical skills. As one owner put it, "The fine dining experience has changed so much: people don't come just to dine, they come to be entertained."

Corporate upscale or casual dining restaurants

These restaurants can be relatively upscale or not at all fancy.

Advantages:

- Security: corporate restaurants are less likely to close tomorrow than a typical independent is
- Often part of a corporate group of restaurants, they offer a chance to transfer closer to home or to move up to a fancier restaurant within the group
- Emphasis on efficient service
- Substantial training likely

Disadvantages:

- They usually keep order among employees by requiring strict adherence to established rules rather than a "we're all in this together" attitude.
- Following protocol is sometimes valued more than providing overall excellent service

HOTEL RESTAURANTS

Hotel restaurants take many forms. They can be fancy and expensive, or casual and cheap. Larger hotels often have one of each type. What we term "hotel restaurants" includes more than the restaurants owned and run by a hotel. In some cases, a restaurant is essentially just co-located with a hotel—leasing space in the same building—but gets much or most of its clientele from the hotel.

Hotel restaurants offer some distinct advantages for servers. At many upscale hotels, guests are either on business expense accounts or fancy vacations, which often means they will be ordering a substantial amount of liquor. Liquor, especially fine wine and drinks rather than beer, raises a diner's tab significantly, which translates into higher tips. In addition, in restaurants owned by a hotel the servers may get substantial work benefits, such as health insurance, 401K plans, and soon. At many chain hotels, you and your family (and possibly even your friends) will get room discounts and other perks at any of the hotels in the group.

In some cases it's easier to get started with a hotel restaurant than another restaurant of comparable stature, because the hotel restaurant may offer a breakfast and lunch shift that does not require as much skill and knowledge as the dinner shift does. As a result, a server can start work on early shifts, learn the food and wine menus, and then transfer to the usually better-paid evening shifts. Do note, however, that in some cities it can be extremely difficult to be hired by a hotel restaurant since the major hotels are unionized. As a result, their restaurants are obligated to hire servers from the hotel staff if any want to work in the restaurant.

Neighborhood restaurants

The term "neighborhood restaurant" includes ethnic restaurants like Italian or Thai, as well as mom and pop varieties. Many follow the traditional formula of dad cooking, mom hosting, and the kids or other relatives serving. It is often much easier to get hired if you are of the restaurant's ethnicity or nationality.

These restaurants usually have an informal atmosphere and can be fun places to work. For example, they often have few articulated policies and are relaxed about servers showing up a few minutes late or eating in front of customers. However, this lack of professionalism may mean that a job at one will be of limited value in getting high end jobs later on.

There are numerous benefits to working in such a restaurant:

- Many neighborhood restaurants recruit employees from local high schools to further their neighborhood ties, making it easier to get hired in your own neigh-borhood—and with comparatively little experience.

- Hiring decisions are often based on current employee recommendations, making it easy to get hired if a friend works in the restaurant.

- You will probably develop repeat customers, given that many regulars frequent these types of restaurants.

- You will probably be expected to chat with customers—unlike in a turn 'n' burn (see page 41).

- Tips will be modest (10—15%) but consistent. You are unlikely to be stiffed by a regular customer.

Disadvantages:

- Only limited training is likely.

- Because many of these restaurants are small, there may be few servers and consequently little opportunity to swap shifts.

- These restaurants are usually slow to employ new technology.

- A substantial number of neighborhood restaurants are under-managed, which can give rise to a culture in which employees take advantage of the opportunity to steal food and liquor.

LOCATION MATTERS

Although restaurants in a chain are meant to be nearly identical, there can be substantial differences among them. For example, chain restaurants located in airports, hotels, or resort towns tend to have a different clientele than those located elsewhere. In an airport, restaurants generally serve much more alcohol than their sister units in the suburbs serve. At TGI Friday, for instance, the norm is for 21–22% of sales to be from alcohol, but at the Pittsburgh airport this rises to 33–35%. The airport customers include many vacationers who are inclined to start their vacations with drinks at the airport, business travelers on expense accounts, and people who drink to calm their fears of flying. All told, liquor consumption can be staggering. Restaurants in resort towns and hotels also serve more liquor than sister restaurants elsewhere.

Location matters in many other situations, too. A suburban restaurant may have a very different clientele, with different consumption patterns (time of day they eat, food they prefer, amount of alcohol they order) from a city restaurant. Even at the micro-level, location can matter hugely. For example, at the Pittsburgh airport, there are two TGIF restaurants. One is busy; the other is ultra-busy. In the former, a server would typically earn $150–200 per shift on $800–1000 in sales. In the latter, a server would make $300 per shift on $1400–1600 in sales. Thus, even at two restaurants in the same chain, serving the same menu, located in the same airport, the tiny difference in location results in a 50–100% difference in server incomes.

So just because you know that serving in one branch of a chain restaurant is unpleasant or low-paying, do not assume this will be true of all branches.

Neighborhood pubs

Many pubs serve a great deal of food as well as alcohol. These can be excellent places to get started. The knowledge required of servers tends to be minimal, so there is relatively little training required to get a new server up to speed. This is particularly true regarding the food menu, which in traditional pubs tends to be rather limited. Not all pubs, however, have limited menus. So-called gastro pubs, introduced to the world by Great Britain in the 1990s, emphasize food more than liquor and often have both more extensive and more exotic food menus. When considering a pub, bear in mind:

- You may be expected to know a substantial amount about different beers, liquors, and cocktails

- In some places you will need to be 21 to serve alcohol

- The atmosphere may be dissolute—full of boozing and drug-taking on the part of customers and/or staff

- Depending upon the nature of the pub, you may frequently encounter bad behavior from drunken customers

- The informality of hiring sometimes translates into the manager or owner favoring a sex partner on the wait staff rather than allocating shifts and stations on the basis of service quality or seniority

Turn 'n' burn restaurants

Diners and their slightly up-market cousins, such as IHOP and Denny's, are frequently unpleasant places to work. Waiters are kept extremely busy:

- They have many tables (eight to ten or more) or counter spaces to serve

- Many of the customers have young (and ready-to-scream) children with them

- Many customers will run servers ragged by requesting innumerable refills of coffee, water, and soda

- Many of these restaurants operate without bussers, so waiters have to bus their own tables

- The side work waiters must perform is extensive because customers run through large amounts of coffee, syrup, salt, and so on

This is not the end of the difficulties. The average bill is low and customers generally tip very little (5—10 percent on average) in these establishments. In addition, the busiest times at many of these restaurants are late night or early morning. Customers may be drunk (and inclined to argue and fight), hung over (and desperate to get some coffee into their system), or just waking up (and grouchy).

On the other hand, these are the restaurants that are most likely to hire an inexperienced server.

Wine bars

Wine bars are generally the exact opposite of a "turn 'n' burn" restaurant. The latter wants to get diners seated, served, and out the door as quickly as possible. Their motivation is to process diners quickly and efficiently and to make the most money possible through the large volume of customers they serve. A wine bar is usually just the opposite. Instead of the servers turning in orders instantly, and the kitchen churning them out immediately, in a wine bar the servers and the kitchen will pace the orders. After the appetizers are served (along with nice wines to complement them), the diners will be given plenty of time to digest and to enjoy and discuss the wines. After a substantial period, the main courses and still more wine will be served. The guests will be unpressured over the main courses, too. The whole experience will be unrushed.

Note how different the pacing is at the two different types of restaurant. The turn 'n' burn is high energy, often almost frantic. The wine bar is leisurely. The two restaurant types call for very different servers. The high energy server who would be perfect for the turn 'n' burn might be dreadful at the wine bar—making mistakes because her boredom makes it hard for her to concentrate, and frustrated that she has so little to keep her busy. And of course the wine bar requires a server to have a substantial knowledge of wine, which might be of limited value in the turn 'n' burn restaurant.

The pace and the nature of the clientele also make for different relationships between server and guest. In the turn 'n' burn, there is little or no time for chitchat with guests, so there is no relationship with them. In the wine bar, however, the leisurely pace and the often elaborate discussion of the wines, and the desire to match wine and food well, encourage and require substantial interaction between server and guest.

BASIC SERVER ECONOMICS

Although other factors, many discussed in this chapter, may affect your choice of restaurant, the money you can earn is likely to be a key factor in your choice. You may be able to find out what servers earn in a given restaurant by asking them. This is sometimes hard to do, however, and even when you can get an answer to this question it's hard to know whether the figure someone quotes is typical. The server might or might not be an average performer, or she might work atypical shifts. She might also want to impress people by quoting the best night's earnings as if they were the norm.

Instead of relying on a server's comment, you can easily estimate how much the average waiter makes at a restaurant if you can find or estimate the following data:

- The average bill per table
- The number of times tables turn (i.e., the number of seatings per shift)
- The number of tables per server section
- The average tipping percentage

In a high-end steak house, for example, this might amount to:

- $450 average bill per table for one seating (3 people at $150 each)
- 1.5 table turnover (i.e., half of the tables have a second seating)
- $675 is the average bill per table for the shift ($450 x 1.5 = $675
- 4 tables per server section
- $2700 is the average sale amount for a shift ($675 x 4 = $2700)
- $540 tip at 20% tip percentage ($2700 x 0.20 = $540)

It may be difficult to get all of this detail, but a few conversations with the servers in a restaurant, combined with your observations from a few meals there, should allow you to approximate the average tips in a shift.

OTHER FACTORS TO CONSIDER WHEN CHOOSING A RESTAURANT

At a restaurant with minimal or low expectations of its waiters, managers often intimidate and push waiters to maintain their standards. At restaurants with high expectations, however, managers don't need to push so hard—waiters and the rest of the staff tend to perform to a higher level because they are motivated by themselves, each other, and the environment.

If you want to work in a high end restaurant with high expectations, look for one that:

- Provides excellent service.

- Offers its servers substantial training.

- Has veteran, skilled waiters you can observe and learn from.

- Cross-trains people in front-of-house roles.

- Runs lean, with relatively few servers compared to the number of diners. All the servers therefore stay very busy, which maximizes tips. This is particularly useful in a "pooled house," because it means everyone pulls his weight.

- Serves a lot of wine and liquor so that the bills tend to be large, thereby generating large tips.

- Takes pride in its service and its food.

- Offers full-time employees benefits, such as medical insurance, vacation and sick time. Note that upscale corporate restaurants are more likely to offer benefits than independent restaurants, with hotel restaurants being the most likely to do so.

Try to avoid restaurants that:

- Have lots of down-time, when you need to be at the restaurant but have little productive work to do. You are likely to be enlisted in tasks such as re-polishing the cutlery rather than making money serving diners.

- Serve a large percentage of unsophisticated foreign tourists unfamiliar with American tipping practices. (See the discussion of Foreign Guests in Chapter 8 for ways to overcome this.)

- Have buffets, since customers at these establishments typically tip little or nothing.

- Have an owner (or manager) who is unable to handle the pressure of running a business. You owe it to yourself not to be disrespected and ill-treated.

In some restaurants, you can pick up and switch shifts (with other servers), whereas at others only management can make these changes. This may matter a great deal if you need a flexible schedule, perhaps because you are a student whose class schedule varies from month to month or a parent who sometimes scrambles to find child care.

Consider the physical demands of the job. If you are required to work four shifts per weekend, you may find yourself exhausted. More than that, this may not be a sustainable pace over the long term. Some restaurants push out older servers because they figure the oldsters cannot—or eventually will not be able to—handle the grueling physical requirements. These are also the places that tend to care little if their employees' health is damaged.

There is a major difference between working at a restaurant that cultivates career servers and expects them to stay for years, and a restaurant that has its servers leave after just a few months on the job. The latter may be fine for a short-term "cash grab," or to get useful experience in the industry, but not for a long-term position.

Note that some restaurants and bars hire, allocate the best shifts, and promote largely on the basis of connections rather than performance. If you lack such connections to the owner or manager, aim to work at places that primarily value performance.

THE DIFFERENCES AMONG BREAKFAST, LUNCH, AND DINNER SERVICE

Good breakfast service often focuses on speed because most guests will be in a hurry. In addition, many guests will be grumpy until they have finished their breakfasts—especially their first cup of coffee—and will not welcome any conversation. Good service requires being efficient and cheerful, but not so bubbly as to annoy anyone. Lunch service differs greatly between two groups: business people in a hurry, and tourists/shoppers with plenty of time. The first group should not have to wait for service; the second group should not be rushed. Dinner service is often less rushed than breakfast or lunch service. Many guests have and want to take the time to enjoy their meals in comfort. There are some exceptions, of course, such as people having to finish their meals in time to get to a movie or play.

Finding a Personal Fit

Most would agree that finding a restaurant where you can earn the most money and be the type of waiter you'd like to be leads to the best personal fit. Ambiance (loud or quiet), pace (measured or manic), and other factors can be important, too. For example, if you don't eat what a restaurant serves, you may not be able to recommend it credibly. This can be a major problem for vegetarians and vegans, not to mention celiac sufferers. In addition, you won't get the full value of the free food a steak house or burger joint offers if all you can eat is the bread or salads.

Politics also can be a consideration at some restaurants, particularly those that promote a cause or attract people of a particular political or social persuasion. If you are a "red meat capitalist," chances are a vegan restaurant won't suit you. The owners, other personnel, and customers are likely to have views diametrically opposed to yours, which is unlikely to endear them to you or vice versa.

Targeting Restaurants Based on Your Skills and Other Attributes

Consider targeting a restaurant in which your second language can be helpful. This is likely to be the case in three different settings:

- The other workers speak this language (which is, of course, highly likely to be Spanish, but may also be Portuguese or some other language depending upon the restaurant and the region). In many kitchens—and by no means just those of Latin restaurants—the language of the kitchen is Spanish.

- The restaurant specializes in the cuisine of this culture. If you speak fluent French, target French, Swiss, or Belgian restaurants.

- The clientele speak a particular language. If Chinese patrons are common and you speak Chinese, that you speak Chinese may be an important selling point for you.

Similarly, your *ethnic background* may be of assistance in getting hired at restaurants of the same "ethnicity." If you are a Korean-American, for instance, you may have a leg up in the effort to get a job in a Korean restaurant. This has less to do with any bias on the part of hiring managers and owners, and more practical matters. Yes, you look the part (which may help create the right ambiance and look for the restaurant), and you will presumably be able to pronounce the names of the dishes and describe them well. Someone with little experience of Korean food and culture would need substantial training and experience to do so.

Much more importantly, in some ethnic restaurants the chefs (and even the owners) speak little or no English, which requires all communication with the kitchen to be in their native language. In these circumstances, nothing substitutes for knowledge of the requisite language.

Interestingly, in a substantial minority of cases, ethnic restaurant managers we interviewed expressed a decided preference for Caucasian servers, largely due to a desire to broaden the appeal of their restaurants. In any event, if you want to work in an ethnic restaurant where knowledge of the local language is not critically important, there are several steps you can take. To improve your chances, learn as much about the food as possible—by tasting it and recording your reactions as well as by learning what each dish's ingredients are and how each dish is prepared. Work on your pronunciation of the dishes and their ingredients. Learn what natives would consider an appropriate combination of dishes for lunch and for dinner. Master the menu of the restaurant you are targeting. Consider learning about the culture's most important feasts. For instance, if you want to work at an Italian restaurant, you could impress the hiring manager by knowing what the Feast of the Seven Fishes is—what it consists of, when it is served, and its cultural and religious significance.

ETHNIC RESTAURANT MANAGERS
DISCUSS THEIR HIRING CRITERIA

"Speaking Italian is a plus, but it's not everything. I would certainly hire someone who did not speak Italian, and was not Italian."

Italian restaurant manager

"Spoken English matters a great deal, but Hindi does not."

Indian restaurant manager

"Being white is a plus in getting hired."

Asian restaurant manager

"Speaking Thai is critical because the chefs speak only Thai."

Asian restaurant manager

"Koreans are easy for us to train; they're accustomed to the food and can pronounce the food names properly. Otherwise, we have to teach (non-Koreans) much more. We also need to give them the opportunity to taste the food so they know how to describe it to guests."

Korean restaurant manager

"New servers need to learn Thai style and culture, including our values."

Thai restaurant manager

"Fluent English is critical. Even bussers need to know enough to respond to a guest's request to get another piece of bread and so on."

Middle Eastern restaurant

"Customers come just before heading off on holiday and want to practice their Spanish—so speaking Spanish is a plus, but not a must."

Spanish restaurant manager

"Some level of Spanish is necessary because the cooks, owners, and others only speak Spanish."

Latin restaurant manager

"Sixty percent of our clientele is Asian, but you can serve them in English."

Korean restaurant manager

LEARNING ABOUT A RESTAURANT

You can get some insight into what it is like to work at a restaurant by consulting employee reviews of it on websites like Glassdoor. But you can and should go beyond this by chatting with servers who currently work at the restaurant. Ask them how many tables they typically have in their section, how much training they received, how effective their managers are, and how collegial the work environment is. What are the main challenges to working there? How does serving there compare with other places they have worked?

Go further and find out what the restaurant is like on different days and at different times. What are the best and worst shifts to work, in terms of both pay and clientele? For instance, Adam worked for a time at a restaurant that was next to a main artery of public transportation and was the only place in the area offering food late at night. As a result, the late-night guests were often rowdy and rude. Dine at a restaurant to see what the service is like; what the demands on the servers are, and how the servers respond to them. Determine whether you could meet the demands and sell the experience the restaurant offers.

AVOIDING RESTAURANTS DESTINED TO FAIL

Try to avoid working for a restaurant that is likely to fail soon. An obvious sign is that it does not do a lot of business. There are also other, less obvious ways a restaurant can fail. A restaurant that is not actively managed is a prime candidate to fail. Without managers on site, or with the managers not holding its servers and bartenders accountable, trouble usually sets in quickly. In some cases, this will mean that employees will steal directly from the restaurant. For example, bartenders may pocket the money for drinks sold, rather than put the cash in the till. In other cases, servers will undercharge or comp their friends or other guests for their meals or drinks. These friends and guests are likely to tip the employees very well for this under-charging. The guest makes out well and the server makes out well, but the restaurant is effectively being cheated.

If you work for this sort of restaurant, you may make a fair amount of money, but you risk developing some very bad habits; you also risk your professional reputation if it becomes known in the restaurant community that your restaurant was a hotbed of questionable behavior.

Note that the restaurants that are most desirable are likely to be hardest to get jobs at—not just because they produce large tip income, but because they select and treat their staff well, so relatively few waiters leave.

AVERAGE RESTAURANT PAY

RESTAURANT TYPE	AVERAGE PAY	EXPERIENCE REQUIRED	ADVANTAGES/ DISADVANTAGES
Fine dining	High	Can be substantial	+ High ratio of pay to work + Waiters treated as professionals
Corporate (upscale or casual)	Medium-High	Can be substantial	+ Training + Useful experience for fine dining
Wine bar	Medium-High	Can be substantial Need to know fine wines	+ Customer engagement + Sophisticated clientele
Neighborhood restaurant	Low-Medium	Little-Modest	+ Relations with regular customers — Limited training, if any — Low tech
Neighborhood pub	Low-Medium	Little	— May need to be 21 — Dissolute atmosphere — Limited training, if any
Turn 'n' burn	Low	Little	— Physically draining — Emotionally demanding — Busiest at odd hours — Limited training, if any

Appendix:
Catering

Catering offers an opportunity for experienced (and sometimes even inexperienced) waiters to earn good money without the stress of a busy restaurant. The work can be uncertain because few catering companies can guarantee you four or five shifts a week, every week, the way a restaurant can. But the hours are predictable: for each catering job, you will be told the starting and ending hours. As a server for a catering company, most of your income will be from hourly pay rather than tips. You will also get free food. (Bartenders get both hourly pay and tips, although the tips tend to be substantially lower than in a regular bar.)

Tasks. What you typically do:

- Set up tables.

- Set up a buffet.

- Pass appetizers while walking amongst the guests.

- Serve from the buffet table.

- Take down the tables and clean up the site.

Requirements

- You may be expected to have some fancy serving techniques, such as being able to use a serving spoon and fork in one hand to dish out something, or to serve wine with a sommelier's competence.

- Because the locations will vary, you need reliable transportation, probably a car or cycle.

There are many advantages to working in catering:

- Guaranteed hourly pay.

- The ability to eat on shift (and often food is available to take home at the end of a shift).

- Relaxed atmosphere.

- Friendly coworkers.

- Variable circumstances: one gig is unlikely to be the same as the prior gig.

- Ease of getting employment. Catering companies are often looking for help, so getting the job (at least in major cities) is not too difficult.

The disadvantages are relatively few:

- Pretentious or privileged clients can be obnoxious.

- Inconsistent work makes it difficult to turn it into a full-time job.

- Pay is only moderate. It's nearly impossible to make massive amounts on a shift when $15 to $20 per hour is the norm.

Suggestions

Since few catering companies are busy enough to provide full time work for servers, you may want to work for more than one. Once you are established at one catering company, ask other servers to recommend you for jobs at the other caterers they work for.

When seeking employment with a catering company, be sure to mention any other special skills you have. Many catering jobs require extensive set-up work unrelated to dining. For example, the caterer for a child's birthday party may need to decorate a patio in a wild west theme. If you have artistic or creative skills, you may be more likely to get the job.

How Servers Are Paid

Servers are generally paid a combination of a basic wage from their employer and tips from customers. The basic wage is usually whatever minimum wage is specified by the city or state the restaurant is in. In many states, the minimum wage is $2.13, the amount specified by the federal government for "tipped" jobs. Approximately two-thirds of states specify a higher minimum wage and some cities also have set their own, higher minimum wages for servers.

The chart at the end of this section shows the state-by-state variation in the minimum wage for servers. Bear in mind that this chart paints with a broad brush. It does not show which cities have higher minimum wages in effect. Neither does it go into detail about exceptions or complications, such as whether the minimum wage for bartenders is higher than that for other servers.

The Basics Of Tipping

Most servers earn most of their income from tips. This is almost invariably true for servers who earn a lot, such as steak house servers who average $300—500 or more per shift.

There are three common ways in which tips are paid to servers:

1. Individual servers keep their tips. This is the most common style of "tipping-out" employees. Each server has a section of the restaurant she is responsible for, and she keeps the tips she receives from these tables. Most restaurants have the servers give a percentage of their tips to hosts, bussers, food runners, and the like, but servers keep the lion's share for themselves. (A typical scheme might give bartenders 5% of the sale of bar drinks; the hostess 1% of total sales; and the food runner 1% of food sales.)

   Pros: If you are a good server, you keep the tips your good service earns you. *Cons:* your coworkers are not inclined

—— 53 ——

to help you manage your section because they do not get a financial reward for doing so.

Implications: In a keep-your-tip environment, you will want to take that last table of incoming guests rather than heading home a bit early. In a pooled-tip environment, you will still get a portion of the tips from the last table even if you don't serve it, so you will be less inclined to take it. However, you should do so when you want to impress your manager with your attitude or when it's your turn (and you certainly want to stay on good terms with your fellow servers).

2. Pooled tips. All the tips servers receive are collected and divided among the employees, with the amount employees receive based upon their job title and number of hours worked. This approach is particularly common in "turn 'n burn" restaurants, which want employees to cover for one another in the often chaotic scramble that is their natural environment. (In some pooled houses (restaurants), new servers earn less than veteran waiters. Thus, in a restaurant with 10 waiters, a new server gets 7% rather than 10% of the tip total initially. In most such cases, the new server's share increases over the course of a year to a full share.)

Pros: In the best of circumstances, a pooled-tip restaurant is a team-focused work environment because every table means more money for every server. Waiters will help one another and thereby make everyone's burden lighter. *Cons:* If you provide great service and your co-workers don't, they make money off of your hard work.

Implications: In general, the less experienced and expert you are, the more you will benefit from being in a pooled-tip environment— assuming the other servers are better servers than you are—because you can learn from their professionalism and share in their higher tips.

3. Tips included in the price of the food and drink. A few restaurants have switched to a European style of pricing that includes tips in the price of the food and drink.

In some of these restaurants, individual servers get the tips that were incorporated in their tables' bills. In most "service-included" restaurants, though, waiters receive a percentage of the total take of the restaurant for each shift they work. The *pros* and *cons* are therefore the same as for pooled-tip restaurants. Note, however, that many Americans will top up the tip, adding an additional tip to the amount built in to the bill. (Foreigners accustomed to the no-tip-necessary practice in their home countries generally will not do so.) Waiters generally keep the extra tips they receive rather than pooling them.

Implications: In no-tip restaurants, waiters are likely to have better relationships with the other staffers, such as cooks and bussers, who often work harder and get paid less than waiters in traditional tipping restaurants.

OWNERS KEEP A PERCENTAGE

Although it is thankfully not common, restaurant owners sometimes keep a portion of the tips left for waiters. It is particularly easy for them to do this when tips are paid by credit card. Sometimes they justify keeping a portion of the tips because of the efforts they undertake to process them. Note, however, that this is illegal in some, if not all, jurisdictions: they are generally permitted to deduct only the actual processing fees that the credit card companies charge.

There is one other "tipping out" practice worth mentioning. In counter service restaurants, there is often a tip jar provided next to the cash register. Tipping is generally very low—nothing approaching the 20 percent in a fine dining restaurant. The generally meager cash tips are divided among employees on the basis of the number of hours worked. Credit card tips, if any, are usually divided weekly.

WHO ARE THE BEST TIPPERS?

The highest-tipping customers are usually regular guests. Close behind regulars are small or medium-sized groups of business people (large groups tend to tip relatively little). However, many of the old rules of thumb—men tip more than women, middle-aged people tip more than the very young or very old, whites tip more than minorities, rich-looking people tip more than those wearing old jeans, and Americans tip more than foreigners—are less useful than they once were.

Three general rules still remain true, however. First, guests' tipping behavior is directly related to their knowledge of tipping norms and customs. For example, many foreigners who are used to having the tip included in the bill in their home countries tend to tip poorly in the United States. Second, if you treat a table as if they are going to stiff you, they probably will stiff you. Third, anyone who has worked as a waiter is likely to tip better than someone who has not. Fellow waiters know that good service deserves acknowledgment, so even if they don't have a lot of money they are still likely to tip well.

MINIMUM SERVER WAGES

STATE/ MINIMUM* STATE/ MINIMUM*
TERRITORY TIPPED WAGE TERRITORY TIPPED WAGE

State/Territory	Minimum Tipped Wage	State/Territory	Minimum Tipped Wage
Alabama	$2.13	Nebraska	$2.13
Alaska	$10.19	Nevada	$8.25
Arizona	$9.00	New Hampshire	$3.26
Arkansas	$2.63	New Jersey	$3.13
California	$12.00	New Mexico	$2.35
Colorado	$8.98	New York	$7.85
Connecticut	$6.38	North Carolina	$2.13
DC	$4.45	North Dakota	$4.86
Delaware	$2.23	Ohio	$4.35
Florida	$5.54	Oklahoma	$2.13
Georgia	$2.13	Oregon	$11.25
Hawaii	$9.35	Pennsylvania	$2.83
Idaho	$3.35	Rhode Island	$3.89
Illinois	$5.55	South Carolina	$2.13
Indiana	$2.13	South Dakota	$4.65
Iowa	$4.35	Tennessee	$2.13
Kansas	$2.13	Texas	$2.13
Kentucky	$2.13	Utah	$2.13
Louisiana	$2.13	Vermont	$5.46
Maine	$6.00	Virginia	$2.13
Maryland	$3.63	Washington	$13.50
Massachusetts	$4.95	West Virginia	$2.62
Michigan	$3.67	Wisconsin	$2.33
Minnesota	$8.15	Wyoming	$2.13
Mississippi	$2.13	Puerto Rico	$2.13
Missouri	$4.73	US Virgin Islands	$4.20
Montana	$4.00		

* Many states also specify that the combination of wage and tips must equal a certain amount. If it does not, the restaurant is legally obligated to make up the shortfall.

Some states have special provisions for employers that provide healthcare coverage, employ more than a set number of workers, or gross more than a particular amount.

Restaurant Glossary

Restaurant Jobs

BAR BACK: whereas the bartender is the face of the bar, making cocktails, serving drinks, and talking with guests, barbacks traditionally restock items, move kegs, and clean.

BUSSER: aids server in serving food, clearing dirty dishes, and cleaning and resetting tables.

CAPTAIN: (in larger restaurants) responsible for service in a large section of a restaurant. He keeps an eye out for any issues that might disrupt the flow of service. For instance, he will step in to help a waiter unable to take an order from a table for a considerable time because she needs to seat an elderly guest whose wheel-chair is malfunctioning.

DRINK RUNNER: aids waiter by bringing drinks from the bar to the table.

EXPEDITER (OR "EXPO"): receives the order ticket from a server and communicates what needs to be cooked to the cooks. May also prepare the final touches to plates, such as adding fries and ketchup to a burger plate.

FLOOR JOBS: jobs in the front of the house, such as server and busser.

FOOD RUNNER: aids waiter by bringing food to the table. The roles of expediter and food runner are almost always combined except in high-end restaurants.

GREETER: greets and seats diners. In many casual restaurants, this is a lower tier, front-of-house job. Generally dependent for earnings on servers tipping them out.

HEAD SERVER: supervises dining room employees for part or all of the dining room.

HOST: (in larger or more formal restaurants) schedules shifts; assigns stations; determines seating; greets guests. In smaller and less formal restaurants, the position is likely to be a mere greeter. Greeters have no power, essentially, whereas hosts function as unofficial managers.

KEY-HOLDER: server or other employee below management level who is trusted with cash management and other financial responsibilities. May be expected to act in a managerial capacity (supervising staff and handling difficult customers) if no managers are on the floor. This position is regarded as a stepping stone to management.

LEAD SERVER: the most senior server on a shift, or in a fine dining restaurant the captain of the table. Lead servers are often responsible for checking the other servers' side work. The lead servers are often the closing servers, too.

MAÎTRE D'HÔTEL (term used in fine-dining restaurants; often abbreviated to maître d') or **HEAD WAITER:** manages the dining room, including determining where to seat guests; oversees the appearance and activities of servers and other staff.

DINING ROOM MANAGER: (in larger restaurants) directs service in the dining room; selects and trains employees; manages budgets and purchasing.

WINE STEWARD (OR SOMMELIER): the beverage and (especially) the wine expert. Creates the wine list, maintains the wine, recommends wine to guests, and serves the wine.

RESTAURANT LINGO

BUSSING: clearing and cleaning a table.

COMP: providing something free of charge, such as an appetizer or even a free meal, usually to compensate for a mistake.

CONDIMENTS: a substance used to flavor or compliment food, such as salt and pepper, ketchup, mustard, and vinegar.

COURSING FOOD: determining how quickly to submit a table's orders. For instance, if a table has ordered a pork chop that takes 15 minutes on the grill and the kitchen is very busy, the pork chop ticket may need to be sent to the kitchen immediately rather than waiting for the appetizers to arrive or be partially consumed.

DOUBLE-SAT (AND TRIPLE-SAT): two (or three) tables seated in one server's section at the same time.

CRUMBER: grooved metal tool used to sweep a table clean of crumbs.

FIRE (AN ORDER): sending the ticket to the kitchen (i.e., placing an order with the kitchen).

FLAG-DOWN: when a customer gets a server's attention, such as by making a signature in the air to indicate she wants the bill, or pointing to the menu because she wants to order.

FRONT OF HOUSE: the dining room, bar, and other areas in which guests congregate or are served (in contrast to the back of house—i.e., the kitchen).

INCOMPLETE PARTY: When one person or couple arrives before the other people who will make up the complete party.

POOLED HOUSE: restaurant in which waiters divide their tips among themselves rather than each waiter keeping her own tips.

SERVICE BAR: area of the bar for waiters to collect drinks

SIDE STAND: storage unit located close to the serving area, where servers keep frequently used items (to avoid having to run to the kitchen constantly)

SIDE WORK: the duties a waiter performs not directly related to serving a customer, such as filling mustard and ketchup bottles, polishing and rolling silverware in napkins, brewing coffee, and so on.

STATION: section of the dining room assigned to a waiter.

STIFFED: to have a table give you no tip at all.

SUGGESTIVE SELLING: used either as a synonym for up-selling (see below) or for the process of getting a diner to order more food, or to choose from a suggested (and limited) list of menu items.

TRAY JACK: a staging device that is set up for servers to put trays on near a diner's table. These are typically tables that fold and are thus highly portable.

TURNING TABLES: serving more than one group of diners at a table during a shift. Thus, if you serve one group at a table at 7 pm and another at 9 pm, you have "turned that table" once.

TURN 'N' BURN: a restaurant that aims to profit by turning tables quickly, with the emphasis on speed rather than a leisurely dining experience.

TWO-TOP (TABLE); FOUR-TOP; SIX-TOP: tables designed for two (four, six) diners.

UP-SELLING: convincing diners to order more (or more expensive) food and drink than they would without your suggestions.

WAITER'S CORKSCREW: also called a wine key or waiter's companion. One of many types of corkscrew, the waiter's corkscrew is a traditional one, with corkscrew, small knife to cut through the foil surrounding the bottle top, and a multi-purpose tool that helps when pulling on the cork.

IN THE WEEDS (OR "WEEDED"): totally overwhelmed; you cannot see through the weeds.

WRITE-UP: management's documentation of an employee's mistake. Write-ups might include documenting poor attitude, sub-par performance, employee absences, and so on in case a restaurant wants to demote or fire someone.

WHERE TO
FIND JOBS

Restaurants use a number of methods to find servers and other employees. The first place most restaurants look is among *current (and past) employees.* Bussers, bar-backs, and hosts often want to become waiters. If you have worked for any length of time at a restaurant in one of these positions, your managers will know a great deal about your attitude and skill, and your likely ability to succeed as a waiter. For restaurants, it is more appealing to promote someone whose quality they know than to take a chance on someone from the outside. Thus, one of the standard ways to become a waiter is to start in one of these less-skilled positions.

A second key source for employers looking to hire is *employee referrals.* Employees tend not to recommend someone who would do a bad job since this will reflect badly on them and also add to their work load. This is particularly true in restaurants in which waiters really like their jobs. Thus, at many high-end restaurants, where turnover is low, the current staff has an important role to play in helping to fill vacancies.

Another common source of referrals is through *customers.* A regular customer who values good service may know of a good server at another restaurant she frequents. Smart managers therefore ask regulars whether they know of someone who would be a good fit at their restaurant. (See the discussion of Networking, below, for more information about cultivating relationships with restaurant insiders.)

Of course, restaurants still *advertise,* whether actively or passively. Their active efforts are no longer confined to the local newspaper (print or online), but now extend to national sites such as Craigslist and local sites. In California, for instance, instawork.com is an important source of restaurant job advertisements; in the Boston area, bostonchefs.com is a valuable source. Poachedjobs.com is an important source in many markets, including Texas and the northwest.

Restaurants may also post ads at local culinary schools and colleges, and even attend local job fairs. (See below for more on job fairs.)

In a more passive fashion, restaurants often devote a section of their own websites to employment opportunities. Note, too, that many restaurants are glad to interview walk-ins during slow periods (usually the mid to late afternoon), even when they do not have any openings. They typically keep these candidates' resumes on file for 3—6 months afterward.

Bear in mind that many establishments other than restaurants hire people to serve food and drink. These include university faculty clubs, caterers, private clubs (such as country clubs), and businesses with on-site dining facilities. So don't limit your searching for job opportunities just to restaurants.

JOB FAIRS

Restaurant companies in need of employees sometimes attend job fairs. These companies may be seeking servers and other restaurant personnel, or they may be looking for people to work in their corporate operations. If the former, you can obviously pitch yourself if the restaurant is the type of place you are targeting. But even if it is not, or it seeks corporate personnel, engage with the representative because he is likely to be well connected in the industry. At a minimum, he can give you advice about how best to proceed. And if he is impressed by you, he can suggest people you should contact or may even offer to forward your resume to them.

NETWORKING

Many restaurant jobs are not advertised; restaurants simply "put the word out" that they are looking for servers. You can learn about these unadvertised opportunities by developing a "network" of people in the industry prepared to keep an eye out for opportunities for you.

Networking is a standard job search technique that involves meeting, getting to know, and helping people who might be able to help you in turn. Although networking for many careers has moved online, useful networking for restaurant work is likely to be mostly or entirely in-person. So rather than focusing largely on our Facebook or LinkedIn or other digital accounts and trying to "meet" people online, devote time to face-to-face meetings in your area (assuming that you do not already have an appropriate network in place).

Your goal is to meet people in the restaurant industry, whether they own, manage, or work in restaurants. You will need to build at least a bit of a relationship with someone before you can expect her to introduce you to people she knows who might be useful to you—let alone to recommend that her restaurant hire you. One way to make this happen is to chat with the people you encounter in the restaurants you already frequent. You can also target restaurants where industry people hang out—particularly the late-night spots that waiters favor. Another way to build a relationship is to find interests you have in common—or to target people whom you know share your interests. So if you love reading manga, watching horror movies, or climbing rocks, look to connect with the people in the restaurant industry you encounter while pursuing those interests.

When building your network, don't overlook your family, relatives, friends, and the people you encounter in your everyday life. They may not work in the restaurant industry, but some of them will surely know people who do. After all, as the introduction noted, approximately half of all American adults have worked in the industry at some point in their lives.

Applying for a Job

Chapter Two

ONLINE APPLICATIONS

Applying for a wait staff position can be simple or quite complicated. A "mom & pop" restaurant might hire you because you are a friend of the owners' daughter. The process might involve just a brief chat—no resume, no cover letter, no reference check. On the other hand, if you apply to a high-end or corporate restaurant, you might have to jump through multiple hoops, including several interviews and a trial shift. This section discusses the latter situation, with an emphasis on the all-important interview process.

Many restaurants, especially larger and corporate ones, will have you begin their hiring process by filling out an online application. The typical application will ask you to provide details of your education: level completed (or number of years of study), diploma or degree achieved, primary area of study, courses taken, and perhaps even your grades (GPA).

For jobs you have held, especially those relevant to working in a restaurant, you will be asked to provide the name and contact details of the employer, your position, the names of your immediate supervisors, your beginning and ending dates of employment, a description of your primary tasks, and the reason for leaving the job.

When completing an application, it's best to emphasize the jobs that are most relevant to your desired restaurant job. Any restaurant work is important to mention as is similar work in a different environment, such as bussing tables in your college dining hall. And any customer service work is relevant, too.

You may also be asked to provide detailed descriptions of specific occurrences during your prior employment, such as a time when you: exceeded expectations, showed a strong team orientation, demonstrated flexibility in responding to an unexpected difficulty, or made a suggestion that management welcomed.

Sample Application Form

ABOUT YOU

_____   _____
NAME   SOCIAL SECURITY NUMBER

_____
PRESENT ADDRESS

_____
PERMANENT ADDRESS

_____   _____   _____
DAY PHONE   NIGHT PHONE   CELL

_____
E-MAIL

Are you at least 18 years of age?   ☐ YES   ☐ NO

Have you ever been employed by our restaurant?   ☐ YES   ☐ NO

Do you have a valid driver's license?   ☐ YES   ☐ NO

If not, will you have reliable transportation to the job?   ☐ YES   ☐ NO
Please describe your transportation plan:

_____

Have you ever been convicted of a felony?   ☐ YES   ☐ NO
Please explain a yes answer:

_____

Are you awaiting trial for a criminal offense?   ☐ YES   ☐ NO
Please explain a yes answer:

_____

Bear in mind that a yes answer to the two questions immediately above will not necessarily disqualify you from employment. We take into account your age at the time of the offense, the nature of the crime, and extent of rehabilitation.

ABOUT THE JOB

Position sought: **Management   Server   Host   Dishwasher   Line Cook**

_____   _____
TOTAL HOURS AVAILABLE PER WEEK   DATE AVAILABLE TO BEGIN JOB

Hours you are available to work each week:

	MON	TUES	WED	THURS	FRI	SAT	SUN
From:	_____	_____	_____	_____	_____	_____	_____
To:	_____	_____	_____	_____	_____	_____	_____

ABOUT OUR RESTAURANT

Have you ever eaten here? If so, please describe your experience, including comments about the food, the service, and anything else you consider noteworthy:

_____

Why would you like to work here?

_____

EDUCATION

Name and address of school	Circle final year completed:	Did you graduate?		Course/ Major	Degree
		YES	NO		
High School	1 2 3 4	☐	☐	_____	_____
Trade School	1 2 3 4	☐	☐	_____	_____
College	1 2 3 4	☐	☐	_____	_____
Grad School	1 2 3 4	☐	☐	_____	_____

EMPLOYMENT (Include jobs most relevant, starting with the most recent)

1.)

NAME AND ADDRESS OF EMPLOYER

Dates of employment _____ _____

TELEPHONE NUMBER   FROM   TO

POSITION   NAME OF SUPERVISOR

PRIMARY DUTIES

REASON FOR LEAVING

2.)

NAME AND ADDRESS OF EMPLOYER

Dates of employment _____ _____

TELEPHONE NUMBER   FROM   TO

POSITION   NAME OF SUPERVISOR

PRIMARY DUTIES
_____

REASON FOR LEAVING

3.)
_____
NAME AND ADDRESS OF EMPLOYER

Dates of
employment _____ _____
_____   FROM   TO
TELEPHONE NUMBER

_____   _____
POSITION   NAME OF SUPERVISOR

_____
PRIMARY DUTIES

_____
REASON FOR LEAVING

May we contact these employers?   ☐   ☐
                                 YES   NO

Have you ever been fired or asked to resign?   ☐   ☐
                                              YES   NO

IMPORTANT ADDITIONAL INFORMATION

Please describe any experience, training, or skills relevant to the position you seek.

_____

Whom should we contact
in an emergency?   _____
                        NAME

_____   _____
RELATIONSHIP   CONTACT DETAILS

How were you referred to us? Employee (If so, who?) _____

Our website Walk-in Employment agency Job fair

Your school Advertisement Other (Specify) _____

FURTHER INFORMATION

Feel free to provide us with any additional information that you think might be relevant to your application. This might involve your hobbies, career interests and plans, or explanations of your educational and employment choices to date.

_____

_____

_____

APPLICANT STATEMENT (Please read the following and sign at the bottom)

I certify that the information provided is accurate, true, and complete to the best of my knowledge. I hereby authorize you to investigate and inquire about this information and related matters as you find necessary.

I release the company, schools, employers, and others from any liability in connection with these inquiries. I understand that providing false, incomplete, or misleading information may result in a refusal to hire me or my dismissal in the event that I have been employed.

I understand that by signing and submitting this application I am authorizing the company to contact the referees listed above as well as my prior employers and schools to verify the information provided.

I understand and agree that if hired, my employment is at will and for no definite period of time. I further understand that I may terminate my employment at any time and may be dismissed at any time without prior notice for reason or for no reason.

_____   _____

SIGNATURE OF APPLICANT   DATE

Cover Letters

A cover letter, along with a resume, was once required in response to nearly any job advertisement. That is no longer always the case, so if you are responding to ads placed by small local restaurants you may need to do little more than submit a resume or fill in an online application form. And if you are targeting a restaurant during its walk-in hours—when people seeking serving jobs are encouraged to walk in the door, fill out a brief form, and undergo a brief initial interview—you may not need a cover letter, either.

The higher up the restaurant quality ladder you go, however, the more likely it is that you will be expected to send both a cover letter (whether an online or paper version) and a resume. Rather than viewing this as a burden, consider it an opportunity. A cover letter gives you a chance to:

- Introduce yourself

- Add personality to your resume

- Demonstrate your knowledge of the restaurant and the position

- Convey your enthusiasm for the job and the restaurant

- Address issues not easily addressed in a resume, such as whether you, as a student, will be available during school vacations

In some situations, a cover letter should be sent even if the restaurant does not require it. For example, if you are following up a networking lead (when someone you know has suggested you contact Jane Smith at the Acme Restaurant), you will of course send her a cover letter explaining how (and why) you came to contact her.

It never hurts to send a cover letter even when its use appears entirely optional. If you are responding to an advertisement that asks only for a resume but does not discourage sending a cover letter, take advantage of the opportunity to personalize your pitch by including one.

The cover letter will often be the first encounter an employer has with you. You can form a good impression if you show that you have taken pains to make your letter appropriate in content and tone and correct down to the smallest details (spelling, punctuation, word choice). After all, employers invariably appreciate a server's attention to detail.

Showing that you can communicate well in writing also strongly suggests that you are well-educated and able to communicate well in general. Both of these are valued in fine dining and many other establishments. Thus, writing a letter that flows logically and is easy to read will work to your benefit.

Since most people communicate only digitally these days, sending a resume and cover letter by traditional (snail) mail may make you stand out. This is particularly useful when applying to high-end restaurants that have innumerable applicants and seek refined professionals, an image your professional letter and resume will suggest of you.

When drafting your letter, be sure to follow these three general rules:

- Keep it short. The letter should be no longer than one page.

- Address it to a specific person, if at all possible.

- Customize your letter, using the restaurant's name frequently. Generic letters suggest it is a mass mailing, which will undercut your message.

The best cover letters use a three-four paragraph structure. The first paragraph tells the recipient what position you are applying for, why, and how you learned about the position. If a specific individual suggested that you apply, mention it in this first paragraph.

Use the second and any additional paragraphs (the body of the letter) to discuss your job-specific qualifications and any transferable skills and experience you may bring from a prior career. Be sure to mention your understanding of what the position requires, and how you've tackled similar responsibilities successfully. Finally, explain why you want to work in this particular establishment. Demonstrate an understanding of the restaurant and its clientele, and indicate why you believe you and the organization are a good fit.

The final paragraph is the place to ask for an opportunity to interview with the restaurant's manager. Be proactive and mention

that you will follow-up with a phone call at a specific time i
of arranging that.

Paper versus online cover letters. If you are sending a paper
of your letter, make sure its appearance (type size and font) is consistent
with your resume and use the same paper stock as you did for your
resume.

Online letters can be a bit shorter than paper versions. If
responding to a large organization's published job ad, include key
words used in the ad because companies often search for these terms
when electronically sorting responses.

When you're ready to hit the send button, either attach your cover
letter and resume with a short e-mail, or put the body of the cover
letter in your e-mail and attach your resume.

Cover Letter Example

Your Name

Address, City, ST ZIP Code | Telephone | Email

Date

Recipient Name Title
Company Address
City, ST ZIP Code

Dear Recipient Name:

I understand from Judy Jones that you are looking for
servers for the opening of your new restaurant, Acme Eats.
Please consider this letter and accompanying resume to be
my application for a position as server.

For the last fourteen months I have worked at Eat Now.
I started out as a busser, but was promoted to server after
just three months. My managers cited my efficiency and
attitude as reasons to give me a try as a server. I believe I
did them proud: after just six more months, I was promoted
to lead server. As such, I have regularly performed closing
shifts, with responsibility for up to ten four-tops.

As you may know, Eat Now is an upscale, but relatively
casual, restaurant. The clientele consists largely of executives

working in the nearby high-rises. It is equally busy at lunch and dinner, with the busiest shifts being Friday lunch and dinner. I have regularly worked five to seven shifts a week, usually including both Friday shifts. Thus, I suspect that my experience maps well onto what working at Acme Eats will involve.

I believe I can be an asset for your restaurant right from the get go. As a former busser and now as a lead server, I have both a strong team orientation and a desire to develop myself and others. I assume that these traits will be particularly useful as you start operations. In addition, I am regularly cited by those who post to Yelp as an outstanding server.

I gather that you are holding open interviews from 2–6 pm on week days .I will come to your premises for an initial interview on Thursday at 3 pm unless you would prefer that I come at a different time. I look forward to discussing my qualifications, interests, and potential fit with your requirements at that time.

Thank you for your consideration.

Sincerely,

Your Name

When Online Forms Do Not Permit a Cover Letter

If you are unable to provide a cover letter, you may still be able to submit a "message" in your online application. This often provides substantial space for whatever you wish to communicate. Consider adding the key elements of what you would have wished to communicate in a cover letter.

Additional Resources

- Ron Krannich & Caryl Krannich, *201 Dynamite Job Search Letters*

- Cover-letters.com. This site includes a large collection of cover, thank-you, networking, and other letters.

Resumes

You will need a resume for most restaurant positions you might apply for. The starting point for constructing your resume is to figure out what your target job is. Rather than writing a general resume that you would use for any job, from retail to restaurant, be specific. Consider the descriptions restaurants use when advertising for servers. If you use these same terms in your resume, you will appear to be knowledgeable about the industry, which will increase your appeal. A resume targeted in this fashion will get you more interviews than a general resume that has no focus.

Once you have selected the criteria that matter most to your target employers, and have learned the phrasing they use to describe them, you can start to match your experience, skills, knowledge, and attitudes to them.

For restaurant purposes, there is nothing magical about the style of one resume versus another. As long as you convey the right information in easily readable (and skimmable) form, you will be fine.

Basic Resume Rules

- Assume that people will spend only thirty seconds on your resume. Therefore, keep to one page.

- Do not stuff your resume; keep it visually attractive and inviting.

- Use a readable 11or 12-point font, such as Times New Roman or Arial.

- Emphasize important points rather than try to list everything you have ever done. Less tends to be more for resume purposes; it shows that you can prioritize and organize.

- Emphasize achievements, providing quantitative or tangible proof of your results whenever possible.

- Show the progression of your career in terms of promotions, increased responsibilities, and the like.

- For jobs you wish to describe in detail, consider separating responsibilities (which you can put in introductory paragraph form) from your achievements (which you can list as bullet points).

- Keep bullet points to one or two lines.

- Make it as up-to-date as possible. Employers tend to be very curious about what you have done most recently.

- Within each category (such as work experience), list items in reverse chronological order—i.e., the most recent comes first.

- The space devoted to the topic should reflect its importance.

- Use "resume-speak"—phrases rather than full sentences.

- Proofread carefully. Have others proofread, too. Remember to remove any tracked changes.

FINE POINTS

- Revise your resume so that it is specifically designed for each employer you target.

- Explain items that are not readily understood by outsiders. The "Night Riders" comes across better as an exercise-promoting evening bike ride than as a group possibly devoted to mayhem.

- Include both paid and unpaid work, space permitting.

- Do not use "I." Rather than "I worked eighty hours per week" write "Worked eighty hours per week."

- Add other categories—Languages, Skills, Personal interests, and so on—as appropriate. High-end restaurants in particular want waiters with sparkling personalities, so showcase any extra dimensions of yourself.

Adam Bronson Murray

999 Acme Road, Berkeley, CA 99999 | (510) 555-9999 | abm-example@gmail.com

WORK EXPERIENCE

2015-16   **Server/Bartender:** *Eureka!*   Berkeley, CA

Learned to manage a section and deal with the stress of working in a turn-and-burn restaurant. Promoted to bartender (2016) but continued to work serving shifts.

2015   **Lead Cashier/Beverage Director:** *Burgermeister*   Berkeley, CA

As Shift Lead/Beverage Director, gained experience working on a register, as well as taking the lead in selecting beers to feature on our taps.

2014-15   **Server/Art Sales Associate:**
Triptych Restaurant and Art Gallery   San Francisco, CA

Waited tables and presented fresh food and wine; managed the stock of wine and beer; and worked with artists to facilitate the sales of their paintings in the gallery setting.

2014   **Library Assistant:** *UC Berkeley*   Richmond, CA

2013   **Stock/Resupply:** *American Eagle Outfitters* Santa Monica, CA

2012   **Server/Cashier:** *Rejuice*   Santa Monica,CA

As one of the first employees, not only handled the cash interactions at the register, but also served customers and assisted the owners with managerial tasks around the store.

2011-12   **Audience Production Assistant:** *Conan on TBS*   Burbank,CA

EDUCATION

2014-16   **UC Berkeley**
B.A. with Honors, in English and American Studies (Double Major)

2009-13 **Santa Monica College**

2009   **Bishop O'Dowd High School** (Oakland, CA)

AWARDS/HONORS

- Wrote and presented a paper at the UC Berkeley American Studies Honors Seminar (2014)
- Honored by Google for work on their Google Books Digitization project at the UC Berkeley NRLF Library in Richmond (2014)

WHAT WE OMITTED FROM THE RESUME ABOVE

The resume printed above is shorter than the one Adam actually used; we truncated it to get it on to one printed page. In the original version, which was printed on a standard size piece of paper, there was room to give several listings fuller treatments:

- The Library Assistant position was described as "Responsible for shelving and paging requested books, as well as working on the Google Books Digitization project and keying in new deposits into the library system." The employer was also listed more fully, as UC Berkeley Northern Regional Library Facility.

- The Stock/Resupply position was described as "Duties included processing new shipments for sale on the floor, filling sales floor with new product, and assisting customers when on the floor."

- The Audience Production Assistant position was described as "Ensured that Conan's live studio audience had tickets and made it to the stage safely.

  Monitored the audience during show times. Traveled with the show when Conan did a week of performances in Chicago. Promoted from position as unpaid intern."

- Also, the Triptych Restaurant and Art Gallery listing had the location on the first line, not the second.

Notes:

Adam highlighted his positions by listing them first, in bold, with the organizations he worked for being listed afterwards. Had he worked for a long string of restaurants, especially if he did so in roughly comparable positions, he would have highlighted the restaurants instead. Thus, his listing for Eureka! would have been:

2015-16 **Eureka! Restaurant**   Berkeley, CA
        Server/bartender

        Learned to manage a section and deal with the stress
        of working in a turn-and-burn restaurant. Promoted to
        bartender (2016) but continued to work serving shifts.

Adam was applying to restaurants in the San Francisco-Oakland Bay Area. As a result, he chose to keep his high school on his resume, even though he had graduated seven years earlier, because it showed his local roots.

RESPONDING TO JOB ADVERTISEMENTS

Some corporate restaurants use software to sort through the large volume of resumes they receive. The software does this by searching for key words that are deemed indicative of a candidate's ability to succeed as a waiter. If you are applying to such an organization, take a look at the ads it is running—and those its competitors use in their advertisements. Glean the phrases used to describe the key requirements for these jobs and use them to describe your relevant experience and background. Do the same in your cover letter, too.

BRING YOUR RESUME TO ALL YOUR INTERVIEWS

Even if you submit your resume in advance, take several copies of it to each interview. Your interviewer may be unable to find the resume you submitted, or someone else may have been scheduled to interview you, only for plans to change. If you have brought copies of your resume, your professionalism will score you points.

Additional Resources:

- Lisa McGrimmon, *The Resume Writing Guide*

- Laurel DeCarlo, *Resumes for Dummies*

- susanireland.com/resume

Interviews

Interviews are a key part of the job application process. A good interview can make up for a lackluster resume, but a good resume will seldom make up for a poor interview. This is all the more the case given the increased emphasis at high-end restaurants on finding servers with sparkling personalities.

Preparation

Your Goals

What you should demonstrate in an interview:

- You understand the nature of the restaurant and the job.

- You are physically able to do the job.

- You have the technical skills and experience to do the job.

- You have the temperament to do the job.

- You want to do the job.

- You are pleasant to work with—and will therefore fit well with the existing team (of servers, managers, and other employees).

- You are manageable—you take direction and criticism well.

- You know what you claim (on your resume or application form) to know.

In general, show that you learn quickly and well, develop your abilities, work well with others, and become very good at any job you take.

Knowing the Restaurant and the Job

Learn as much as possible about the restaurant and the position:

- Know the history of the restaurant, its typical customers, and its major competitors.

- What are its opening hours? When is it busiest?

- What is it noted for? What dishes are most popular?

- What is the pace of the work? How many tables do servers cover?

- Are there bussers? Food runners?

- Know how to pronounce everything on the food menu and wine list.

- Review which dishes you know. Practice describing them. Look up the dishes that you do not know. Learn their ingredients and how they are prepared.

- Consider what appetizers and side dishes you would suggest diners add to each main course.

- Be ready to describe the beers they offer, especially any local brews.

- Examine the wine list. Where do most of the wines come from? What is the price range of the whites? Of the reds? Which would you recommend with each main course?

- What is the clientele? Who dines there at breakfast? At lunch? At dinner? Where do they come from (the neighborhood, nearby office buildings, etc.)?

- What are the major challenges servers face? The pace of work? The knowledge to satisfy a sophisticated clientele? (Or perhaps something less attractive, like drunken customers?)

- What is considered appropriate attire for servers?

To gather this information, speak with people who currently work there and former employees. If possible, visit the restaurant yourself to observe both servers and customers.

DO ADDITIONAL HOMEWORK

If you are particularly keen to get a job at a specific restaurant, consider increasing your relevant knowledge of its specialties. For example, if you have targeted an oyster bar, read either or both of Rowan Jacobsen's excellent books, *A Geography of Oysters* and *The Essential Oyster*. If your target restaurant has a large cheese offering (as many wine bars do), read the fine book by Max McCalman and David Gibbons, *Lessons for Connoisseurship from a Maître Fromager*. In addition to impressing the hiring manager with your knowledge, you will have demonstrated your willingness to invest effort to improve your capabilities.

Match your Experience and Skills to the Requirements

Once you know the job's responsibilities, consider what you have done in the past that will help you perform them. Include in your consideration the transferable skills and attitude that will help you. For instance, the job may involve serving wine snobs and you may not have any customers of this sort. However, you may know French food and wine terms because you studied French. Similarly, you may have worked at a cigar shop that served similar customers—very fussy about the cigars they bought—and, as a result, you needed to learn about the various expensive cigars sold there. Your mastery of French and familiarity with a similar group of customers suggest you should be able to handle this job.

ANTICIPATING THE QUESTIONS

Many restaurants will put successful candidates through two or three interviews. The first one will be a screening interview designed to eliminate those who are clearly not suitable in order to focus more carefully on the serious candidates. Many restaurants will use a brief telephone interview as a screening device to determine which candidates to invite for a face-to-face interview.

First interviews are likely to involve:

• Filling out an application (if you have not already done so)

- Logistics issues
  - Do you want to work part-time or full-time?
  - What would be your preferred shifts and hours per week?
- Answering relatively straightforward questions, such as:
  - (Assuming you have had experience) How did you start serving?
  - Why would you like to work here?
  - What do you know about this restaurant?
  - How have you learned about it?
  - Who (if anyone) referred you?
  - What relevant experience do you have?
  - Why are you considering leaving your current employer?
  - What are you best at? Worst at?
  - What are your favorite parts of your current job?
  - What would be the ideal work environment for you?
  - Are you hoping to work for months, years, or decades at your next job?

Second interviews are likely to probe more deeply:

- You may be asked to walk your interviewer through your resume—explaining each relevant job you have had
  - Why you took the job and why you left it
  - The nature of the restaurant (or other employer)
  - Your responsibilities (and how they changed over time, if you were on the job for a considerable period of time)
  - What you did well or less well
  - What you liked and disliked about the job
  - What you learned from it
  - Why you intend to leave your current job

- Hypothetical questions, to test your experience, commonsense, and ability to handle stress. For instance, what would you do if...

  · A crying child disturbed diners at other tables?

  · A guest wanted to send back a perfectly good bottle of wine?

  · Your busser was lazy and did not pull his weight?

- Specific questions about your experience: which shifts did you work, how many tables did you handle, whether you've served wine, and so on

- Specific questions about your skills and knowledge

- Where do you want to be in five years? Ten years?

- Your attitude

  · Enthusiasm for the job

  · Enthusiasm for the restaurant's concept

  · Desire to serve

  · Desire to learn

- Fit with the restaurant's image, culture, work style

- Are there any physical or other limitations that would hinder your performance?

- When would you be able to start?

Other Questions to Prepare For

- Why do you want to be in the restaurant business?

- How do you take direction?

- How would your current boss describe you?

- What are your current boss's greatest strengths? Weaknesses?

- Tell me about a disagreement you had with your supervisor and how it was resolved.

- What special qualities or talents would you bring to this job?

- What has been your biggest contribution to your current employer?

- What is the best constructive criticism you have recently received? How did you respond?

- What is the most important thing your next boss could do to improve your performance?

- (To determine your teamwork inclinations:) Tell me about your experience on athletic teams or in other groups, as well as how you have managed conflict with colleagues.

- Tell me about a conflict you have had on the job, and how it was (or was not) resolved?

- Tell me about a crisis you had to face on the job, and how you did (or did not) handle it?

- What do you do differently now from what you did in your first weeks as a server? (i.e., what have you learned to do better?)

Another Way to Anticipate the Questions

Many interviewers have a standard way of conducting interviews, including the questions they ask. Thus, a manager may always ask an applicant what she knows about the restaurant, why she is considering leaving her current restaurant, and what her greatest strengths as a server are. If you can speak with one or more people who have interviewed with that manager, you may be able to learn exactly what questions to expect.

PRACTICE

There are two ways you can practice your interviewing skills and response. The first is by doing mock interviews with someone who has appropriate experience in the restaurant business. Ideally, this would be someone such as a restaurant manager or owner who has interviewed servers for his restaurant. However, it could also be someone who is hoping to apply for similar jobs. Your interview partner can tell you which responses were convincing and which were not and why. Be persistent and push your interview partner to be specific in noting what worked and what did not. Speaking out loud often makes it clear that you are wandering instead of staying focused, trying too hard to excuse some prior mistake, or pleading rather than persuading. Recording your practice sessions will make this apparent.

The second way of practicing is to interview with a restaurant that matters relatively little to you. This allows you to develop and refine your pitch and get rid of your first interview nerves without too much at stake.

It is a good idea to use both of these approaches if you can. Maximize the potential benefits by debriefing your partner after an interview, or reviewing the experience yourself, to be sure you understand what worked and what needed more thought, and why.

Physical Preparations

Physical Energy

Energy is important for service. Even if you look appropriate, you will need physical and emotional energy to provide good service for long periods. Be sure you have taken appropriate steps to appear energetic in your interview.

- Get plenty of sleep the two nights before the interview.

- Eat a solid breakfast or lunch on the day, so that you do not run out of energy.

Appearance

- Arrive at the actual site slightly before the allotted time so that you do not need to rush and get nervous as a result. Find the restroom and check your appearance closely.

- If there is a chance you will have ruined an item of clothing (shirt, stockings) immediately before the interview, perhaps during your shift at your current restaurant, consider carrying an extra one with you.

What to Bring

- Take copies of your resume and a copy of your application form (if any), even if you submitted them prior to your interview. (The person who interviews you may not have been given copies, or may have misplaced them.)

- Have the name, telephone number, and email address of your interviewer in case you need to contact her to notify her of a delay in your travel.

DURING THE INTERVIEW

A considerable degree of the impact you have in an interview is achieved nonverbally; nonverbal messages typically constitute over half of the message you deliver. As a result, it is highly appropriate to consider such factors as dress, behavior, and the like in order to maximize the chances of interview success.

Appearance

Interviewers will make assumptions about you in the first few seconds they see you. These assumptions will color how they evaluate the whole interview. Their initial judgment—partially conscious and partially sub-conscious—will be based on the way they expect a professional server to look. Thus, the more up-market the restaurant you are gunning for, the more your sophisticated your appearance and demeanor should be.

- Wear clean, neatly pressed clothes.

- If your shoes are the type that can be shined, do so.

- Be sure your clothes fit well.

- Avoid wild colors or styles (unless you know they will be appreciated by a particular restaurant).

- Cover up any tattoos and remove piercings to the extent possible (unless you know they will be appreciated by a particular restaurant).

- Be sure your hands, fingernails, and hair are clean and

well groomed. (The significance of this for fine-dining restaurants cannot be emphasized enough.)

- Do not wear any cologne or other fragrance.

- Be sure you have invested appropriately in mouth-wash, deodorant, and other hygienic necessities. If you smoke, do not do so in or near your interview clothing.

Note that some of the owners and managers we interviewed preferred that candidates go beyond this and dress like they would for an executive position in a corporation—suit and tie for men, the equivalent for women.

Behavior

- Greet the interviewer with a smile, an extended hand, and a positive handshake (matching the interviewer's pressure). A firm handshake conveys confidence.

- Look the interviewer in the eye. Eye contact conveys honesty.

- Do not smoke, drink, or eat anything even if invited to do so— not even if the interviewer herself does. This can distract either you or the interviewer, perhaps showing you to be clumsy or worse, without any chance of improving her opinion of you.

- Do not chew gum.

- Be sure your cell phone is turned off.

- Maintain good rapport with the interviewer by being warm and smiling often. Do not, however, smile idioti-cally without stopping for the entire interview.

- Sit up straight, but not rigidly, and lean forward slightly. This will show that you are interested in what the interviewer has to say.

- Listen carefully and show that you are listening by nodding, or saying, "uh-huh," "I see," or "right"occasionally.

- Avoid crossing your arms, or folding your arms behind your head.

- Move as gracefully as you can. One of the key factors being assessed is your physical coordination.

Speech

- The goal is to sound confident, mature, friendly, and professional.

- Speak at a normal speed; do not rush.

- Avoid conversational tics such as frequent use of "like," "you know," and "um."

Attitude

Be upbeat. Emphasize your strengths. Do not discuss your weaknesses in any detail unless pushed to do so.

Relax and enjoy yourself. The relatively few people who enjoy interviews are those who view them as a chance to discuss important matters with an equal who happens to be interested in the same subjects. They view the interview as a time to learn more about the restaurant and job as well as a chance to explain themselves.

Look interested. Avoid looking at your phone or watch. Do not stretch in your chair. Do not appear bored, no matter how long the interviewer is speaking. If you are shown around the restaurant, be sure you exhibit great interest in what may be your future place of employment.

YOUR TIME TO ASK QUESTIONS

Many interviews, especially final interviews, conclude with a chance for you to ask questions. Failing to ask questions if you're invited to do so risks leaving the impression that you either did not do your homework or do not particularly care whether you land the job. Asking questions gives you the opportunity to show how knowledgeable you are about the job and the restaurant—and that you are taking a proactive approach to your career.

Questions you might wish to ask:

- How long have the other servers worked here?

- How long is a typical diner's visit?

- What is the typical profile of a lunch guest? A dinner guest?

- What do you consider most important in a server?

- When waiters do not work out, what is the most common reason?

- Who succeeds in this job? Why?

- Do you expect the restaurant to change much in the near future?

- What do servers particularly appreciate about working here?

If you are particularly keen to land the job (and have the nerve to ask a leading question), you might ask:

- Do you have any questions or concerns about my desire and ability to do the job? If so, can I address any of them?

- I'd love to do this job. Can you picture me working here?

If, in spite of the suggestions above, you have no questions to ask, you can always fall back on the old standby: "I had a number of questions when the interview started, but you have covered all of them."

TESTING YOUR SKILLS

If you have made it this far in the interview process, you may be asked to perform a trial shift, to see whether you can perform as expected. This will include how you treat the guests and your prospective colleagues. (See page 105 for more about trial shifts.)

Another way a restaurant may test you is to ask you to "sell" various items from your current restaurant's menu to your interviewer. The quality of your descriptions, your ability to answer questions about the items, and your poise and enthusiasm can all be judged through this exercise.

Ending the Interview

Smile at the interviewer, shake hands, and thank her for seeing you, then leave with an energetic, confident demeanor.

Follow-Up

After your interview, send a thank-you email or letter. Mention something in the interview that was personal or unusual. Sending a traditional letter (by physical mail) will make you stand out.

General Rules For Interviews

Do not criticize others without good reason. Even if you have good reason to criticize your former colleagues or managers, do not let the focus of more than a small part of the interview be on your criticisms. Otherwise you may be viewed as a chronic complainer. Remain positive.

Do not take over the interview. Interviewers want to feel they are in charge of an interview, since they need to feel confident that they will be able to get the information most relevant to their decision-making. Taking over the interview may allow you to make the points you want, but the risk is too great that your interviewer will react very negatively to this and resent your aggressiveness.

Answer questions concisely. Do not ramble. Do not take more than two minutes for any but the most involved, important questions. In fact, three to five sentences is an appropriate length for the majority of answers.

Listen well. Be sure you have understood what the interviewer is asking. If uncertain, ask for clarification of the question. Answering the question you thought was being asked, or the one you anticipated being asked, rather than the one she really did ask you, will annoy her and suggest that you are either dim or not paying attention. Listening well means more than paying attention to what is being said. It also requires that you encourage the interviewer by appearing interested.

TOP TEN INTERVIEW TIPS

- Arrive on or ahead of time
- Appearance: neat, clean, and professional
- Attitude: positive, confident, open, and friendly
- Smile and make eye contact
- Engage comfortably with your interviewer—as you would with a diner
- Show energy and eagerness to work hard
- Show flexibility and eagerness to learn
- Know a lot about the restaurant, and why you want to work there
- Be ready to tell your story, with an emphasis on how much you love serving and love working in a team environment
- Be genuine: let your pleasant and engaging personality shine through

TELEPHONE INTERVIEWS

Telephone interviews are a cost-effective alternative restaurants often use in place of traditional face-to-face interviews. They're usually conducted on a pre-arranged schedule, so you are unlikely to have to worry about an unexpected call catching you by surprise. Although the questions you will be asked over the phone are no different than those you would be asked in person, telephone interviews are still sufficiently different from in-person interviews to require some specific advice.

Preparations

- Even though the arrangement for the call is likely to be made by email or text, be sure your voicemail message is suitably professional just in case.

- If you live with others and share a phone, let them know that you may receive a call from a restaurant and make sure they will respond politely if they happen to answer the call.

- Try to use a landline if possible. This way you can avoid the propensity of cell phones to drop calls, break up, or go mute, all of which is likely to annoy your interviewer.

Have Available

- A pen and paper to jot down notes. Do not use a computer because the sound of typing can annoy the interviewer by making it seem like you are multi-tasking rather than focusing on the interview.

- Your resume.

- Your notes about the restaurant and position, boiled down to the key points you want to recall or communicate.

- A glass of water, in case your throat goes dry.

The Call Itself

- Take the call in a quiet place where you won't be interrupted or distracted.

- Do not put the call on speaker. Doing so makes it hard for your interviewer to understand your responses.

- Speak directly into the telephone, keeping the mouth-piece about an inch from your mouth.

- Do not try to read prepared responses. It is highly likely that this will be apparent to your interviewer, which will call your abilities into question.

- Even though your interviewer won't be able to see you during the call, your location and posture will affect your performance. If you are slumped on the couch, your voice will probably be weak, you'll mumble rather than enunciate clearly, and you will seem timid, uninterested, and antisocial. On the other hand, if you stand and wave your free hand about, you will probably come across as dynamic and engaged. And if you smile, it will make you sound engaged and upbeat.

Practice

- Phone interviews are very different from in-person interviews, in large part because you cannot see how the interviewer is reacting to what you are saying. Without the ability to receive the usual cues from the interviewer's body language, eye contact, and the like, many interviewees lack the confidence to give full answers and resort to truncated, even yes or no, answers. In order to practice and get used to speaking without such feedback, conduct multiple mock interviews by phone.

- On the telephone, the rhythm and tone of your voice are particularly important. To learn what you sound like, consider taping an interview (with the permission of your volunteer questioner). Listen for your enthusiasm, voice level (try not to whisper or shout)—as well as the substance of your responses.

VIDEO (ZOOM OR SKYPE) INTERVIEWS

More and more restaurants are making use of video interviews. Video interviews combine some of the best aspects of telephone and in-person interviews. They can be done without expensive and time-consuming travel and both parties can see one another, thereby adding to the sense of connection and reality that telephone interviews generally lack.

Although video interviews can be seen as a cross between in-person and telephone interviews (and the advice offered regarding both, especially telephone interviews, should be consulted), some elements are different and call for specific advice.

Preparations

- Dress as formally as would be appropriate for an in-person interview to show you are taking the interview seriously. Don't wear stripes or busy patterns because they are likely to be blurry and annoying to the viewer. If possible, avoid wearing white (which reflects light). Instead, opt for a pastel shirt or blouse (blue is an excellent choice).

- A plain backdrop works best. Avoid having anything distracting on view, whether on your desk or on the wall; clean up clutter. Similarly, make sure there are no childish or embarrassing items visible.

Practice

- Most people are very stilted the first time they do a video interview. Practice can overcome this. Even so, it is extremely difficult to know how you are coming across to an interviewer. To learn, have a friend do a two-way session with you in which he or she records your efforts.

- Check your internet connection as well as your microphone and camera settings—and do so again an hour or so before your actual interview.

- Sit a little more than arm's length from the computer/camera.

- Have your interview partner check to make sure you can be heard, your face and torso are visible (and your face is in the middle of the screen, with your eyes about two-thirds of the way to the top of the screen), and there is nothing distracting in view (on your desk or the wall).

Technical Issues

- Do not assume that your computer's built-in microphone and camera are up to snuff. Test them and determine whether you will need to upgrade by buying a microphone or headset (to avoid speaker playback) and an attachable camera.

- Set up the camera so that your head, shoulders, and torso are centered in the frame and clearly visible. If you sit too close to the camera, you will show just your head, which would make it seem too large and eliminate the body language that flows from the rest of your body.

- Good lighting is important. The goal is to have your face be well lit. During daytime you can use daylight from windows, but make sure the light is in front of you, not to the side or behind you. At night, have a lamp in front of you, aimed a bit above your eyes.

The Call Itself

- Do not watch yourself on the computer screen. Look at the camera instead, so that the interviewer will sense you making eye contact.

- Try to make a connection as you would with an in-person interview. Read your interviewer's expressions and body language.

- Do not be wooden. Gesture naturally, including with your hands, but don't move forward and backward much.

- Smile as much as you can.

- Do not be surprised if there is a sound delay. If so, pause before answering a question.

- If you are interrupted, how you handle the interruption may tell a great deal about you. For instance, if your baby brother comes into the room and starts whining that he wants your attention, being able to deflect him gracefully (and perhaps with a little smile and shake of the head) will reflect well on you. Screaming at him to get lost will not.

- At the end of the call, you cannot stand up and shake hands, but you can still find a gracious way to end. One way to do so is to say, "Thanks so much for interviewing me. I enjoyed it." Smile and nod your head.

Follow-Up

- You have little excuse for failing to send the interviewer a thank-you note, since Zoom and Skype make it simple to leave your interviewer a message. Be sure to do so shortly after the interview.

INTERVIEW EVALUATION FORM

A typical interview evaluation form notes the personality traits, attitude, motivation, and experience that a restaurant looks for, and asks the interviewer to provide a numerical rating of a candidate along with comments meant to expand on that. A typical form for a fine dining restaurant would be:

FACTOR	1 = POOR	10 = EXCELLENT
Appearance	Disheveled, dirty, unprofessional	Neat, well groomed, professional, attractive
Attitude	Negative, unsmiling. Impatient at having to answer questions	Positive, upbeat, smiling. Pleased to respond to questions
Motivation	Little interest in the job	Keen to work for us and needs to work
Drive	Drifts from day to day	Sets high targets for own performance & improvement
Communication	Inarticulate	Able to chat easily with our clientele
Responsiveness	Avoids giving specific answers	Answers questions with appropriate specificity and detail
Desire To Serve	Cares little about guests	Born to serve
Poise	Easily rattled or upset	Maintains poise even when highly stressed
Knowledge of Our Restaurant	Knows next to nothing about us	In-depth knowledge of who we are & how we operate
Technical Skills	None; would need substantial training	Highly skilled; little or no training required
Experience*	Non-existent	3+ years in similar position in similar environment
Personality**	Poor ft for our environment	Good fit for our environment

Overall Rating (out of 110 possible points)

* Some restaurants would not include experience as an important factor in their evaluation.

** Many restaurants would list key personality traits that they would wish to evaluate, such as friendliness, dynamism, and so on.

TATTOOS AND PIERCINGS

Older generations of Americans view tattoos and piercings differently than younger generations do. For many older Americans, tattoos are meant to be limited to sailors, prisoners, and side-show circus freaks. Many studies show that tattoos are linked in their minds with smoking, drug and alcohol abuse, general criminality, and violence. At the very least, they are seen as signs of rebelliousness. And the bigger the tattoo, the more older folks fear that the person bearing it is not to be trusted. This is also true for tattoos of any size on the face, neck, and hands.

Younger Americans—40% of whom have tattoos—tend to view the matter differently. This generational divide is also mirrored to a lesser degree by a socioeconomic divide: wealthier folks living in conservative areas of the country are more likely to be bothered by tattoos than less wealthy folks living in hip areas of the country.

The various views of tattoos have major implications for servers looking for employment. Those applying for work in hip San Francisco or Manhattan bars are unlikely to be disadvantaged by a display of their tattoos or piercings unless they are extremely pronounced or otherwise worrying. However, the more conservative the area, the fancier the restaurant, and the older and more conservative the clientele, the more likely it is that an inked or pierced candidate will be at a disadvantage. This will of course vary according to several factors, including how visible and how aggressive the tattoos and piercings are.

Rather than rely on these generalities, try to visit restaurants you have targeted as potential employers to see whether the servers have any visible ink when in uniform. If they are all wearing long sleeves, they may be conforming to a restaurant policy of covering up tattoos.

Then consider how you would feel about covering up your own ink or piercings (if this is even possible). If you cannot cover them up, or choose not to, bear in mind that many independent restaurants—especially beer-driven restaurants or bars that do food service—gladly hire inked and pierced servers. However, many of these more liberal establishments may balk at someone sporting tattoos that are racist, sexist, vulgar, or threatening, or piercings that might make their customers squirm.

ELEVATOR PITCH

When trying to land a serving job, whether in a formal interview or when you bump into the owner of a neighborhood restaurant, you should be ready to give a concise pitch for why you should be hired. This is your "elevator pitch," a term derived from the idea that this is what you should say if you found yourself alone with the person in charge of hiring at your target company on an elevator that would take only a minute or two to reach her floor.

Given that people speak at approximately 120–150 words per minute, you can convey a great deal in your brief—approximately 60 second—elevator pitch. Think in terms of why a restaurant should hire you. Start developing your pitch by answering the following questions:

- Who are you?

- What do you know about this company and this position that makes you want to work there?

- What relevant experience do you have?

- What skills have you developed?

- What attitudes and values do you possess and have you demonstrated in your work?

Adam's basic elevator pitch before working at Zazie was this: "Although I've only recently graduated from college, I've had very good experience as a waiter, bartender, and cashier, most recently at Eureka. I've consistently been given increased responsibilities wherever I've worked. I'm attracted to [name of restaurant] because of its reputation for excellent food and, most importantly, the team spirit in the front of house. I think I'd be a great addition to the team because of my extensive and successful experience with teamwork, both in school and at work. In addition, I've always been a great communicator, and I take criticism well, so I think I would be able to adapt quickly to your well-run operation. I should emphasize that I WANT TO WORK and am happy to pick up shifts that others want to get rid of."

KEY PHRASES TO USE IN AN
ELEVATOR PITCH OR JOB INTERVIEW

- Please, thank you, you're welcome
- I love interacting with guests
- I get great satisfaction from pleasing guests
- I'm energetic and work hard
- I work well with others
- I definitely want this job

Practice your elevator pitch over and over. Write it out, read it out loud, read it in front of the mirror (making sure you look confident when doing so), and then practice it with your family and friends. You need not be word perfect, but by the time you expect to use it, you should be able to put across your key points easily and without hesitation or stumbling.

MANAGERS AND OWNERS
GIVE INTERVIEW ADVICE

PREPARATION

"Showing that you've done your homework is a little thing that goes a long way in an interview—you know the menu or something unusual mentioned on the restaurant's website. The fact that you've put in the time and effort to learn about the establishment says a lot about your character—it suggests you're willing to make an extra effort."

Fine dining restaurant manager

"Know the restaurant: the chef's bio, what we stand for (using local farm produce)."

Hotel restaurant manager

"Know something more about the restaurant than just where to show up for the interview."

Fine dining restaurant owner

"Know the history of the restaurant and what it's known for. If you can, try some of the food."

Fine dining restaurant owner

APPEARANCE—
ESPECIALLY FOR UPSCALE RESTAURANTS

"When it comes to your appearance, three things matter most: you have shaved, you are smiling, and your nails are clean. If not, you don't care about your image, and you haven't worked in a fine dining place before (because you would not have gotten away with this), and you are not clean."

Fine dining Italian restaurant manager

"The first impression is critical: they need to be clean-cut and well groomed."

Steak house manager

"I hate the nose rings, tongue piercings, sloppy dress."

Fine dining restaurant owner

"Dress like you're going to a corporate interview. Don't think that because it's the hospitality sector that you can dress casually."

Fine dining restaurants' owner

"The first impression matters a great deal. I pay particular attention to his grooming—how is he dressed? Has he shaved well?"

International fine dining restaurant manager

"Good posture is incredibly important."

Corporate casual chain manager

"I don't like candidates showing up wearing extensive jewelry or makeup, or designs on their nails. But a good smile can overcome some of these issues."

Fast casual restaurants' owner

"A person absolutely must be well groomed."

Seafood restaurant manager

"A smile is part of your uniform."

Fine dining Italian restaurant manager

"Things I pay attention to: what time a candidate arrives, how they are dressed. In addition, their hair and nails should be well groomed."

Upscale casual restaurant chain manager

References

Most restaurants expect you to provide at least two references, preferably from current or past employers. Although references from your prior restaurant managers are most valuable, you can still profit from nearly any reference that discusses favorably your reliability, team spirit, diligence, flexibility, and work ethic. Even if you have demonstrated these attitudes and values in a retail setting, they will also be prized in any restaurant setting.

Choosing Recommenders

If possible, it's always prefer to choose a person who has supervised and evaluated you in a similar position. Ask whether he or she would be willing to act as a reference for you before giving their name to a potential employer. If he or she is willing, go beyond that to make sure she will be supportive of your candidacy and will talk about your work ethic, reliability, and so on in a positive light. Ask what sorts of things she would be happy to say about each of these topics. Take notes; you will want to be able to mention in interviews the sorts of things your recommenders will likely say about you.

Alerting Your Recommenders

When a restaurant indicates that it will check your references, notify your recommenders to expect a call and brief them regarding:

- The job you are seeking
- The sort of restaurant you are applying to
- And why you have targeted this restaurant (or restaurant company)

When checking your references, the restaurant may ask for only a little information or for a lot. If the restaurant wants a lot, the following are the types of questions likely to be asked:

- Can you confirm her dates of employment?
- What was her position?
- How long did you supervise her?

- What were her responsibilities?
- What did she do well? Poorly?
- What should she work to improve?
- How well did she get along with managers? Colleagues? Customers?
- How closely did you need to supervise her?
- How punctual was she?
- How often did she miss a shift?
- How motivated is she to perform well?
- How much did she improve during her time under your supervision?
- What was the most important critique or suggestion you gave her? How did she respond?
- How did her performance compare with that of her colleagues?
- In what kind of work environment would she be at her best? Her worst?
- Why did she leave your restaurant? Did she provide suitable advance notice?
- Would you be willing to re-hire her? Why or why not?

Or a recommender may be asked to rate your performance on a 1–5 scale along the following dimensions:

- Punctual
- Reliable
- Honest
- Hard-working
- Attentive to detail
- Friendly
- Team-oriented
- Consistent (vs. temperamental)
- Skillful
- Professional
- Calm in spite of stress
- Organized

LIKELIHOOD YOUR RECOMMENDERS WILL BE CONTACTED

Some restaurants check references as a matter of course; others do so only occasionally. In general, the restaurants most likely to check references are those hiring people not already known to them in some manner (for example, by referrals from current staffers) and those that have many candidates to choose from. In some cases, the nature of the candidate occasions a reference check. If someone claims experience that seems unlikely ("I was the lead server at age 19 at the fanciest restaurant in town"), a reference check may result.

Overall, restaurants are checking references much more often than they did in the recent past.

CLEANING UP YOUR ONLINE PROFILE

Do not be surprised if your would-be future employers also do a social media check on you. This check can be far more extensive than just looking at your current Facebook account. So if social media has been part of your life—or that of your friends (who may have posted captioned pictures of you)—do an in-depth search of your name and see what pops up. If your late night rant about your ex, drunken dancing on a Tijuana tabletop during spring break, or other embarrassing elements of your past show up, clean up whatever you can. Change your Facebook and LinkedIn profiles and get your friends to take down offending pictures of you.

Trial Shifts and Probationary Periods

Trial Shifts

Once a server's resume and interview have passed inspection, many restaurants give potential employees the chance to show their abilities by working a trial shift. A trial shift is typically two to four hours long. If you have had relevant experience you may be expected to help a veteran waiter or waitress serve a few tables or, after a briefing on how service is to be performed at that restaurant, you may be given one or two tables to wait on yourself without assistance. Your performance will probably be judged on the following criteria:

- Are you proactive in figuring out where to get condiments, where everything is placed, and so on?

- Are you highly organized—not having to rush back and forth between the kitchen, the service station, and your tables because you forgot things?

- Do you engage pleasantly with the diners?

- Do you get along and fit in with the other employees?

- Do you exude enthusiasm? Are you keenly interested in pleasing the diners?

- Are you active—not just watching what others do or chatting with other waiters?

- Are you good at whatever you claimed on your resume and in your interview?

If you have not had experience working as a server, you will probably be asked to shadow a server and perform simple chores such as pouring water, setting tables, clearing plates, and the like. You will be judged on the basis of how well you perform these simple tasks, how you speak with guests and staff, and how quickly and well you learn things. And, of course, exhibiting a pleasant demeanor and willingness to work will also be critical to your success.

PREPARING FOR A TRIAL SHIFT

Eat one or more meals at the restaurant before your trial shift. You can see how tables are set, where servers get condiments, how waiters approach tables, what opening phrases servers use, whether waiters write down orders or just remember them, and more. Knowing these things will allow you to focus on the diners you are serving rather than worrying about all of the mechanics that could distract you from engaging with them.

Note that some restaurants no longer use trial shifts to determine whether a server meets their standards because they fear the liability exposure if a non-employee is injured or causes an injury to someone else.

Probationary Periods

Many employees start work at restaurants on a conditional basis. This probationary period, which is usually thirty to sixty days long, allows managers to evaluate potential employees' attitude, skills, and development. If the employee performs well, she will be usually given the job on a more permanent basis. If not, she will be let go.

Employees who have been working at a restaurant for some time can also be placed on probation if they are not performing well or have violated restaurant policy in some way. This probationary status is often used as a warning—"you need to shape up"—and as a potential prelude to firing someone for poor performance.

Appendix: Standard American Table Settings

Formal Dinner Table Setting

Butter Spreader

Bread & Butter Plate

Water Goblet

Red Wine

White Wine

Napkin

Salad Fork
Dinner Fork
Dessert Fork

Soup Bowl

Service or Dinner Plate

Soup Spoon

Teaspoon

Dinner Knife

Informal Table Setting

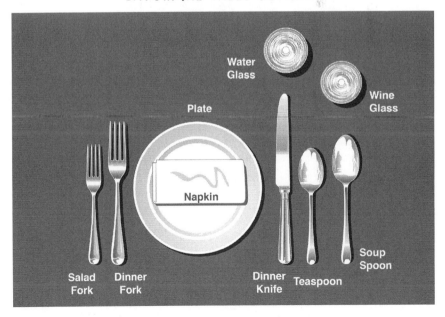

Water Glass

Wine Glass

Plate

Napkin

Salad Fork

Dinner Fork

Dinner Knife

Teaspoon

Soup Spoon

Breakfast Table Setting

Getting Started

Chapter Three

First Steps

When You Are Offered the Job

Once you have an offer on the table, make sure you fully understand the compensation package you are being offered: pay, health insurance, vacation policy, and any other benefits. It's also important to fully understand the restaurant's expectations of its employees. For example, if you are signing up with a large or corporate restaurant, you may be given a copy of its employee manual and then, once you have had a chance to read it, you will be asked to sign a statement that you have indeed read it, understand it, and agree with its terms. Once you have done so, the restaurant can hold you to the policies described in the manual. For example, if the manual specifies that male waiters are not allowed to have beards, then you should shave yours or risk losing your brand new job.

When a restaurant offers to hire you, you need to be ready to start immediately, and to work whatever shifts you said you would be able to handle. It would be good, too, if you could offer to work any other shifts, to demonstrate your ready-and-willing attitude to your new managers.

Once You Are Hired

To get started on the right foot as a new employee, you will need to:

- Make sure you know the procedures for your first day of work: when you should show up, what you should wear, who you are reporting to, and so on. Be sure to arrive extra early on your first day.

- Learn the names of your colleagues.

- Learn the menu thoroughly. Learn what substitutions are possible. Learn the drinks. Learn the seating.

- Be available for the first month without needing to take any time off for any reason.

- If at all possible, leave your cell phone behind. Get used to making and answering calls on your own time, not your employer's.

While the prospect of learning all you need to know to be an excellent server may seem daunting, you can at least professionalize your appearance and personal cleanliness with relative ease.

YOUR APPEARANCE

Appearance matters in a service business, and is especially important in the restaurant business. You are the face of the restaurant—the one interacting with the paying customers. You not only influence what customers order; you also do something rather intimate—have physical contact with their food and drink.

Dress

Make sure you look clean, professional, and appropriate for your restaurant and its clientele. Your clothing should:

- Be very clean and, in the case of your shoes, shined. Guests don't want their food handled by someone messy. It's usually a good idea to keep an extra shirt, tie, or jacket at the restaurant to replace whatever may be soiled during your shift.

- Fit you well and be free of wrinkles

- Not be suggestive (unless, that is, you are working in an environment that encourages blatant sex appeal, such as some cocktail bars and Hooters-style establishments)

In addition:

- Your shirt should be tucked in (unless you are working in a hip restaurant with a very relaxed dress code)

- Your undies (and rear end) should never show, no matter how far over you bend

The ideal style of dress will vary by restaurant. In some cases, your dress will be mandated, such as in restaurants where all servers wear black trousers and a white shirt (or blue jeans and black t-shirt). If the choice is up to you, presumably you will aim for something that:

- Flatters your figure and coloring (hair, eyes, skin)

- Is comfortable

- Reflects both your personality and the personality of the restaurant

No matter what sort of restaurant you work in, bear in mind that customers prefer a neat and tidy person rather than a shabby-looking one.

Buy enough uniform pieces (shirt or blouse, trousers or skirts) that you always have a clean outfit available. Many servers have only one or two of each and consequently often show up in soiled clothing.

Cleanliness

- Cleanliness is critically important in the restaurant business. Diners do not want to be served by anyone who neglects their personal hygiene.

- Be sure your hands look clean. Take extra care that your nails are clean and in top form. Most restaurants prefer servers to keep their nails short and evenly trimmed. Wash your hands frequently, including after you blow your nose or use the restroom.

- Your hair needs to be clean and, if long, should be tied back in some fashion. Dropping even a strand of hair on a customer's food is likely to upset him.

Keep your section clean. When you arrive at the restaurant, inspect your section to make sure it is spotless. This includes the floor, the table, the chairs, and everything on the table. Make sure the cutlery and glassware are clean and polished, without food, watermarks, lipstick, or anything else on them.

Odor

Dining is meant to arouse all the senses, olfactory perhaps most of all. If you have just downed a cup of coffee, or eaten garlic or onions, use a mouthwash and/or brush your teeth.

The smell of smoke can be very off-putting for those about to eat, sometimes even if they are smokers themselves. If you smoke and don't have the chance to shower and change your clothes before your shift begins, at the very least brush your teeth and wash your hands afterwards.

Perfumes and colognes are best avoided, because even a modest aroma may clash with the food—and will certainly not enhance it.

Training Programs

Many restaurants hesitate to invest in extensive training for their servers because they suspect many waiters will end up quitting in the near future and the restaurant will not benefit from the cost and effort they put in. These restaurants favor the "learning by doing" approach. Other restaurants put a bit more effort into training their new waiters by having them shadow a veteran waiter for a shift or two. However, there are some restaurants that take a more proactive approach to training. This is true of some independent restaurants, especially upscale ones. It is even more true of corporation-owned chain restaurants. The four corporate restaurants highlighted* below were chosen because they are well known national chains but focus on very different fare, and have clear guidelines when it comes to training their servers.*

- *PF Chang* (Asian cuisine). PF Chang's training program starts with five days in a classroom setting learning the culture, food, recipes, and standards of the restaurant. This is followed by five days "on the floor." New hires start with positions they were not hired for, but which they need to understand. They work as a host for a day, busser for a day, and bartender for a day. They then shadow a server for two shifts. After this, they do a "mock" service where they serve the managers. This service is done on a start-stop basis, with managers stopping them to correct or alter whatever is necessary. Only after they complete this training are they allowed to wait on tables themselves.

- *The Cheesecake Factory* (Mixed American cuisine). The two-week training program at The Cheesecake Factory resembles that of PF Chang. New servers spend their

* These descriptions of the restaurants' training are based on our interviews with their managers.

first week in the classroom developing knowledge of the recipes used for each of the many menu items. They also learn the technical part of the job from an experienced, or "elite," trainer, such as how to greet tables and the various steps of service. In the second week they receive "on the job" training. They shadow a server for their first two shifts. They increase their practical knowledge, such as at which kitchen windows different food items come out, the table numbers in the restaurant, and so on. They follow a server as she greets tables, allowing them to watch what it's like to interact with guests. Next, they are given two tables to serve while an experienced server shadows them. Then they are given three tables. On their final day of training, they are observed by a designated server, who watches them through their whole shift and grades them in detail.

• *McCormick & Schmick's* (Seafood restaurant). Here, training consists of working five shifts. At first, a new hire shadows a waiter, then she serves together with a waiter, and then she serves while being watched by an experienced waiter. Finally, she serves a manager. Once she has done this successfully, she serves actual customers on her own. If she has had a year or more of experience in an upscale casual or fine dining restaurant, she will be given dinner shifts to work. If she has not had such experience, she will start with breakfast and lunch shifts. These are less demanding, so she has the chance to develop her skills and knowledge (of the menu and of wine). After a few months, she may be judged ready to work dinner shifts.

• *The Capital Grille* (Steak house). The training process is the same for all new servers. Each works one shift as a host, then a shift as a server's assistant, and then a shift as a food runner. After that, the new hire works three to four shifts shadowing a veteran server. Passing that test, the new hire "goes live," serving tables alone, for two weeks. This two-week period is an opportunity to hone technique and develop the flourishes that provide the fine dining experience the restaurant seeks.

In well-run restaurants, training does not end once an employee finishes the initial formal training program. Instead, periodic briefings or refreshers address issues that have arisen, new and better ways of serving, changes to the menu, and so on. Some managers encourage continuing skill and knowledge development through other techniques. Several we spoke with require that one or more servers "sell" them on two or three specific food or drink items before each shift starts. This keeps servers' knowledge of menu items up to date as well as requiring them to practice their selling techniques in front of their colleagues.

Those who want to get a running start as new servers, or who want to develop their skills to the utmost, stand to benefit greatly from an extensive training program.

ALCOHOL-SERVING CERTIFICATION

In some states and cities, those who sell or serve alcohol must take a Responsible Serving-Alcohol Server Certification course. This generally applies to bartenders, servers, and possibly others who will come into contact with alcohol, such as food runners and bussers. This requirement can usually be satisfied by taking a brief, online course. Where such certification is required, your restaurant is likely to help you pay to acquire it. (Many restaurants pay a blanket fee, covering all of their personnel, for the relevant course.)

Other Ways To Get Your Foot In The Door

As we have discussed, you will probably be able to get a job waiting tables even if you have little or no experience. But what if you cannot? What if your background or geographic location works against you? For instance, perhaps you have been in and out of employment for an extended period. Or quite possibly your area is economically depressed and serving jobs are hard to come by.

If so, you may want to consider working in another position in a restaurant and using it to transition into a wait staff position. You can start as a hostess, busser, or bar-back—or possibly as a food runner or expeditor. None of these jobs pay as well as waiting tables does, but they are useful stepping stones on the route to becoming a waiter. Note, too, that this approach will work if you have targeted a high-end restaurant serving position, knowing that it would pay a great deal, but the restaurant won't hire you. Perhaps it has no positions open. Or it only hires from its roster of current employees, preferring to train up a busser familiar with its operations rather than bring in a server from outside. In this case, you may want to work in a non-serving position at the restaurant to qualify for later employment there as a server.

Other Restaurant Roles

A *host* or *hostess* is the first employee a guest encounters. As such, she is the face of the restaurant. Her duties include:

- Responding to phone calls

- Giving directions to people coming from nearby hotels or across town

- Greeting guests in a welcoming manner

- Helping diners with their coats, umbrellas, and bags

- Establishing and maintaining the reservation list

- Quoting correct waiting times and keeping guests updated as the waiting list evolves

- Seating guests at the correct table

- Thanking the guests for coming and expressing a desire to see them return soon

- Helping people call a taxi or other transportation, particularly if they have consumed too much alcohol

An effective hostess needs to handle guests showing up late for their reservations, people acting badly if they have to wait for a table, and the chaos that occasionally envelops all but the best-run restaurants. She needs to deal with all sorts of guest complaints, and remain courteous and respectful in all situations.

This position involves a great deal of interaction with guests, which means that the ideal applicant has an outgoing personality, a friendly and attractive appearance, and good posture and grooming. She is articulate, well-spoken, and probably an extrovert. Perhaps because this position does not involve serving alcohol, many restaurants use students and minors as hostesses.

A *busser* does the grunt work in serving a table, clearing it after guests have finished, and cleaning up both the table and the surrounding area. Typical duties include:

- Pouring water and coffee, bringing bread and butter

- Removing dirty utensils, glasses, and dishes

- Clearing and cleaning table when guests leave

- Preparing the table for the next set of guests—setting it in the restaurant's chosen manner

- Keeping the area clean and neat

If there are no food runners and the waiters are busy, a busser may also bring food to the table.

A *bar back* is expected to do everything for the bar short of making drinks and accepting payment. Duties include washing glasses, stocking ice, getting liquor and barrels of beer from the basement, emptying the trash, and so on.

A *food expediter* receives order tickets from servers and tells the cooks what needs to be cooked. An expediter also finishes plating the food, such as adding tartar sauce and lemon to a fish entrée, and making sure the resulting plate looks aesthetically pleasing. A *food runner* takes the food to the tables. In many restaurants, the two positions are combined. And even when they are kept separate, as in some fine dining restaurants, a seasoned food runner should be able to perform the duties of an expediter and vice versa. Note that these two positions are more likely to require previous restaurant experience than the other three are.

Transitioning to the Wait Staff

Working in any of these positions can offer you the opportunity to impress a restaurant manager with your effort, teamwork, ability to stay calm in the face of stressful conditions, willingness to learn, and eagerness to become a waiter. Here are ten tips to impress managers with your readiness to become a waiter:

- Perform your job well.

- Work hard—take on extra work rather than avoiding it.

- Learn to be organized and efficient, rather than rushing about frantically.

- Maintain a winning attitude: smile and appear pleased with your work.

- Stay as neat and clean as possible.

- Ask to cross-train in other positions, especially front-of-house positions.

- Pay attention to what servers do, and be ready to duplicate their actions.

- Find an experienced waiter willing to give you pointers.

- Volunteer to take any available shifts as a waiter and, when given the chance, perform to the best of your ability.

- Show yourself as articulate and knowledgeable about the restaurant's offerings and operations in conversations with your manager, fellow employees, and guests.

Gaining Work Experience In a Café

If times are tough and you cannot get a job in a restaurant, you can probably get a job in a café such as Starbucks. Although working behind a counter is not the same as waiting on tables, it is similar in many important respects, including:

- You will deal with all kinds of people.

- You will have to multi-task.

- You will interact with other workers in serving customers.

- You will need to learn to remain unflappable even when handling a crowd of thirsty and impatient customers.

- You will have the opportunity to engage with some customers who like to chat.

- You will become accustomed to working with a standard computerized entry system.

An Indirect Approach

Yet another possibility is to get a job as a *mystery diner*—someone who dines anonymously at restaurants and reports on the nature and quality of the food and service received. Large restaurant companies employ mystery diners as a way to keep track of how well their various restaurants are performing. You can learn a great deal about how guests assess service. That said, this job will not get your foot in the door of a specific establishment. You will not be able to demonstrate your energy, team orientation, connection with guests, and table-waiting skills. As a result, working as a mystery diner will probably not advance your efforts to become a waiter as much as the other jobs discussed in this section will.

Moving Ahead

Chapter Four

Mastering
Your Craft

In your first serving job, try to master as many of the basics as possible:

- How to greet guests and make them feel welcome.

- The ingredients used in each dish and how each dish is prepared.

- Basic cooking terminology (braised, poached, sautéed, simmered, stir-fried, deep-fried)

- Tasty ways of describing dishes.

- Knowing which dishes can be prepared to meet dietary restrictions.

- How to use the technology the restaurant uses to take orders, place them in the kitchen queue, and calculate a bill.

- How to read what guests want—the tempo of the meal, whether and what type of suggestions to offer, the appropriate degree of interaction and formality.

- How to take orders and how to ring them up.

- How to stock your side station.

- Serving children—and keeping them satisfied and entertained.

- Knowing when to put in drink, appetizer, entrée, and other orders.

- Restaurant lingo and your restaurant's abbreviations.

- Serving (and removing) food and drink items properly—from the appropriate side, for instance.

- Loading both food and cocktail trays correctly.

- Arm service—carrying food or drinks without a tray.

- Folding napkins in several artful ways.

- Standard table settings—where the knives, forks, spoons, plates, glasses, and cups are placed—for breakfast and for dinner.

- How to work as a team with a busser.

- What sort of glass is used for each drink—and what goes in it (different garnishes, for example)—so that you can help the bartender by setting glasses up.

- Serving wine.

- How to handle more guests at any given time.

- How to present the check.

- How to manage rude or inebriated guests.

In addition to these basics, it can be helpful to learn the ropes of other positions with the restaurant so that you can step in, if necessary. Even if a restaurant does not cross-train employees, consider volunteering for a few shifts (or shadowing someone) in another role in order to learn it thoroughly.

Much of your mastery will come from experience, but some can come from reading about how to handle various matters. Thus, if you work for a restaurant with a waiter's manual, read it carefully. A typical manual will cover dozens of key topics.

Some of the following tips are fairly basic, whereas others are advanced—and may be less important in very casual restaurants.

General Demeanor

Letting your personality shine is likely to work well for you, *if* the real you that comes through is upbeat and positive.

Making eye contact and smiling convey warmth and establish rapport. Smiling actually influences you to be more positive and it also influences your guests to like you more.

Standing tall, with your shoulders back, conveys ease and confidence.

Avoid behaviors and habits that may make your customers uncomfortable. Nervous habits such as nail biting are obviously taboo when you are on your shift. Even chewing gum is considered unacceptable in all but the most casual and easygoing restaurant environments (and sometimes even there). So try to break yourself of any gum-chewing habit you may have—especially if you chew with your mouth open or "crack" your gum.

Before Guests Arrive

Before customers arrive, do your "side work," the essential duties beyond the actual serving of guests. These include learning the specials for the day (and whatever is on the menu but unavailable due to food shortages), preparing the tables in your section, and stocking your sidestand. A well-stocked sidestand may include children's menus, bibs, coloring books, and so on; a large range of condiments, including steak sauce, horseradish, Worcestershire sauce, various mustards, etc.; clean and folded napkins; water pitchers; and on and on.

Prepare coffee machines and fill water pitchers. Make sure the salt and pepper shakers are filled and their openings not clogged. Clean the oil and vinegar containers. Dust crumbs off chairs.

When your restaurant is not busy, such as between mealtimes, don't just chat with your fellow servers. Instead, prepare your tables: make sure the chairs and tables are clean (and not wet or sticky) and not wobbly. Make certain that your tables have the required settings. Make sure that the silverware and dishes have no food on them. If there are cups or glasses, make sure there are no lipstick or lip gloss marks on them. And record information about guests you have recently served that you want to remember. (See page 220 for more about this.)

Pre-Shift Meetings

Some restaurants hold pre-shift meetings to convey important information to the staff, perhaps in combination with exhortations to work hard or have fun. In these meetings managers will typically mention:

- The day's specials.

- Which menu items are unavailable, usually due to shortage of key ingredients but sometimes due to a problem with kitchen equipment or staff.

- Which menu items the restaurant wants you to push, due to an over-supply or the items nearing their sell-by date.

- Staff assignments—who has what station.

- Staffing issues—if someone has failed to show up for a shift, how others will need to cover for him or her.

Many waiters and other personnel consider these meetings a near waste of time and behave accordingly—rolling their eyes, paying little attention, and generally making it obvious that they consider the meetings beneath them. Unsurprisingly, this greatly annoys the managers. You should treat these meetings as learning opportunities and, by so doing, you will impress your managers with your attitude.

Listen attentively to what your manager is saying and participate as appropriate. Ask questions to be sure you understand everything. Accept criticism of your performance gracefully. Solicit suggestions for how to provide better service. Don't blame others for any failures on your part. Think about how the team as a whole can perform better.

GREETING GUESTS AT YOUR STATION

How you greet guests when they first arrive at your station can have a strong impact on their dining experience, not to mention your tip. If you greet a group with a perfunctory hello, you are making it clear that they can expect no better than minimal service from you. On the other hand, if you greet them warmly, they will anticipate good service and a positive dining experience.

Greet customers with a smile and "Welcome" or "Good evening, welcome to [name of your restaurant]." Try your best to make customers feel good—welcome and special. In fact, it's always a good idea to go beyond just a "Good evening" greeting. "Good evening, I'm delighted you've come for dinner." Or, "Good evening; it's wonderful to see you again." Your warm welcome can of course be either quite formal or informal, depending upon the nature of your restaurant.

If you are uncertain how many guests there are, ask "How many are in your party?" If there may be just one person, ask "Table for one?" instead of saying "Just one?" or "Are you alone?" The latter two phrases suggest that the solo diner is somehow wrong in dining alone. Some single diners, especially women, can feel awkward about dining alone. If you ignore them, you will add to this feeling. Do what you can to make them feel welcome. Bear in mind that single diners are often business travelers, which means they are on an expense account and thus likely to spend a good deal. Assess whether the guest wants to be left alone to read or work, or would like to chat a bit to overcome any feeling of solitude.

When you know a customer by name, greet her with it, but always formally unless that individual has said, "Call me Mary." If your customers introduce themselves (presumably in response to you introducing yourself), remember their names and address them by name. But do not ask their names, which is likely to seem too forward.

If you have an "incomplete" party—where one or two guests have arrived before the others who will join them at their table, take advantage of the opportunity. Ask the one who has arrived the names of the other guests—so that you can tell the hostess whom to expect. In so doing, you can also learn his name (because the guests may be asking for him by name) and/or the name in which the reservation, if any, was made. Tell the hostess whom she should expect, but be alert to those guests arriving yourself. If you see them arrive and are not otherwise tied up, you can greet them by name, give your name, help them with their coats and bags, and escort them to the table. "Mr. Smith, your colleagues have arrived." This gives you the chance to deliver high quality service and in so doing learn a whole set of names and thereby improve your chances of converting them into regulars.

Try to establish a rapport and start learning your guests' mood and interests. (See the Appendix for more about "reading a table.")

Simple Rules to Follow

Before seating guests, make sure the table is ready. This means that the table, dishes, silverware, and glasses are clean, and the table does not wobble.

Always aim to greet the table within a minute of their arrival. This will allow them a few seconds to settle in, without a risk that they will worry that they might have to hunt for their server. If you are busy serving another table, you need to stay focused on that table. However, you can also make it clear to the entering customer that you have seen him and that you will deal with him shortly. You can do this with a nod, eye contact, a mouthed or spoken "I'll be with you shortly." Acknowledging a customer in this way suggests to him that you will not dawdle in your current task and will instead get to him as soon as possible.

The ten-five rule: if you are within ten feet of a guest, make eye contact and smile. If you are within five feet, greet and welcome him.

Once all the guests in the party have been seated, remove any unused place settings.

Taking Orders

The traditional signal that a guest is ready to order is that she has closed her menu, but not everyone does this; some like to browse the menu even when they have decided on their order. When taking an order, make eye contact with your guest. Doing so will suggest that you are giving her your full attention; it will also be taken as an indication of your trustworthiness.

Note whatever items on the menu are unavailable (due to having run out of something, for example). Then mention the specials and their prices, speaking at a moderate pace so that diners can understand and evaluate them.

Whether to Write Down an Order

It's admittedly impressive when a waiter can remember a complicated set of orders without having to write them down. Doing so also eliminates the time required to take notes. It's therefore understandable that some restaurants forbid writers from writing down orders. However, when you are just starting out, we suggest you write orders down if you have the option to do so. You will make fewer mistakes this way—and will not annoy diners by having to check and re-check what they ordered. In writing down the orders you can easily note which seat is associated with which order. (This is particularly useful if a food runner will deliver the food, because he can read your order form and quickly know which seat at the table gets which items.) Otherwise you need to make a mental note of this—and then verbally pass this on to the food runner if you will not be serving the food yourself. In any event, you want to avoid having to auction the food when it arrives at the table—"Who gets the chicken? How about the fish?"

If your restaurant does not use written guest checks, your guests may be worried that you will not be able to remember their orders correctly. One way to reassure them is to repeat their order to them— word for word. This will be particularly important in settings where the loud music, conversation, or television can cause mistakes.

Getting the Orders Right

Now is the time to ask whatever is necessary to get the orders right:

- How should the meat be cooked? (Rare, medium rare, medium, medium well, well done)
- What is preferred on the potatoes, butter, sour cream, or something else?
- What type of salad dressing is desired? On the salad or on the side?
- What side vegetable is preferred?
- The toast: wheat, multigrain, or white? Dry or buttered?
- Always confirm orders with any dietary restrictions.

It is usually a good idea to try to take care of children first. If they are unhappy or just hungry, they can spoil the meal for the adults— and anyone else within earshot. Ask the adults at the table if they would like you to order the children's meal first and get them started quickly, or if their meals should be served at the same time as the rest of the order. Be patient with the children (and their parents), and try to help them feel contented and occupied. Smile at them as if they are very cute (whatever the truth may be).

SUBSTITUTIONS

Many diners will want to substitute for the items accompanying the main course. Perhaps someone has ordered fish and chips but would like to have something green rather than the French fries. You should know what you can substitute automatically—without having to ask a manager for permission to do so. This may include a green salad or green beans, for instance. Similarly, someone may want a starch other than mashed potatoes. Know whether you can offer roast potatoes, French fries, rice, or something else.

You can also improve your service by knowing what special items—particularly good-looking vegetables, for instance—have just arrived and can be substituted.

Learn, as well, what can be ordered as a half portion, and what the price of a side dish would be if ordered in entrée size.

SPECIAL DIETS, ALLERGIES, AND RELIGIOUS RESTRICTIONS

Many guests will be allergic to one of fourteen allergens, especially nuts, eggs, milk, shellfish, fish, and wheat. You should know which menu items do and do not contain these and other key ingredients. Other guests will be trying to maximize or minimize something in their diets. The following are common issues:

Gluten free. Some customers will try to avoid wheat, but getting trace amounts of it will not be a major matter for them. Celiac sufferers, however, are so allergic to wheat that even the smallest amount can make them sick for days. So you should know what on your menu, if anything, is suitable for someone who needs to avoid even a hint of wheat. (Note that some foods that you may not think of as "wheat" nonetheless have plenty of it, such as soy sauce.) Know, too, what menu items can be fixed in a gluten-free fashion. Discuss this with your manager and chefs.

Healthy choices. Many guests will want to avoid calories, fat, sugar, salt, carbohydrates, processed food, particular oils, and so on. If you know both what ingredients are used and how items are cooked, you can help steer guests to foods that will meet their requirements. For instance, what cooking oil is used for the sautéed chicken dishes?

POINT OF SALE SYSTEMS

No matter where you work, it's likely you will need to become used to using one or more point of sale (POS) computer systems. NCR's Aloha system is the most common POS system in the U.S. at the moment, and luckily it is quite easy to use. Revel Systems and others are creating iPad-based POS systems that are very intuitive to use. Expect to see more of these in the coming years. Smaller restaurants without a full POS may use Square to process credit cards.

A good POS system:

- Takes orders by seat. (Seats are typically systemized in north-south-east-west terms.)

- Notifies the waiter of any special deals.

- Adjusts prices by day part (lunch vs. dinner) or day of the week.

- Collects loyalty information if the restaurant tracks this.

- Dispatches the order to the kitchen, typically through a kitchen display unit (KDU).

- Notifies the waiter and her team when the food or drinks are ready.

- Allows the bill to be split by person, by percentage, or major item (e.g., "split the food three ways and add the wine to my bill").

- Allows the waiter to document guest preferences (the man prefers green tea to coffee).

Timing the Orders

In the restaurant business, good timing equates to good service. Always aim to get entrées on the table shortly after guests have finished their appetizers. In some cases, this will mean you need to put in their entrée order at the same time as their appetizer order; in other cases, you will want to wait until they have started their appetizers to order their entrees. For instance, if the slow-cooking entrée will require 30 minutes to cook, and their hummus appetizer will appear within a minute (and take a modest amount of time to eat), you should certainly order the entrée at the same time as the appetizer. If the reverse is true—the appetizer will take time to consume and the entrée will be ready quickly, you will want to wait to put in the entrée order.

Serving

When the food comes out of the kitchen, make sure the order is complete, including any sides dishes ordered. If any additional cutlery (soup spoons, steak knives) is required, collect it before serving the table. Give yourself bonus points if you make sure each plate is attractive (well-arranged and without stray food, especially sauces or gravies).

If the food may require pepper that you will grind on it, bring the pepper grinder with you.

The main item, usually the protein (meat, chicken, fish, or whatever), is placed in the 6 o'clock position—directly in front of your guest. Other food items are placed to the side or behind this. The reason is that this item is generally both the primary focus of the diner and the trickiest item to cut. Positioning it at 6 o'clock allows the guest to cut it without having to reach across other food and risk a sleeve sliding across the salad and getting coated in dressing.

Know what each guest has ordered so that you do not need to auction the food ("Who ordered the brisket?"). As you serve the food, check again to make sure that everything has arrived—side dishes, additional cutlery, and so on.

Once you have served the food, check back with your guests to make sure everything is as-ordered and see whether there is anything else they would like. They may want to have a soup spoon to eat a non-soup item, hot sauce for their rice, or who knows what. Time your check-in with the table so that your guests have had a chance to taste the food first. A traditional rule of thumb is: "in two minutes or two bites." If a guest has to wait to get a fish knife to eat her fish, and the whole table waits for her to start, the meal can be ruined if it takes five minutes for her to catch her server's eye.

Wait to ask how guests like their food until they have actually tasted it. Do so in a manner that aims to get an honest response rather than a robotic, "It's fine." If anything is amiss, deal with it immediately.

As a general rule, serve kids first, and women and elderly diners next (unless guests indicate to the contrary). Keep the table as clean as possible. Guests feel taken care of when they are in a spic-and-span environment.

Many customers think that drink refills are the definition of good service. Do not let refillable drinks (water, soda, iced tea, coffee) run out, but do not go to the opposite extreme of re-filling glasses every two or three minutes. Recognize, though, that coffee is a special case. Regularly offer coffee refills, but do not actually pour the coffee until the guest assents. The reason to hesitate is that the guest may have the right balance of coffee, milk, and sugar at the moment, which will be upset with the addition of more coffee. (Or she may want to limit the amount of coffee she will drink but recognize that if coffee is put in her cup she will end up drinking it.) If a guest's coffee has had time to cool, consider replacing her warm coffee with a fresh cup.

Get drinks to your customers as soon as possible after they've been ordered. Customers find it extremely frustrating to have to wait for a drink. This is especially true if they order wine and it has not arrived by the time the appetizers appear. Note that the better your relationship with the bartenders, the more likely your drink orders will be processed quickly.

Clearing

Replace dirty silverware, including any that has dropped on the ground, with new silverware.

Do not attempt to remove a guest's plate when others at the table are still eating the same course.

Do not ask whether you may remove a plate the second someone has finished eating from it.

Rather than asking, "Are you still working on that?," ask "Shall I remove that plate?" Suggesting that someone is "working" on her food rather than enjoying it is off-putting.

If you remove a dish that is still loaded with food, politely ask whether there was something wrong with it.

MAINTAINING CONTACT WITH DINERS

Nothing is more frustrating for diners than being unable to find their waiter when they need something. Make sure that when you are serving one table, or walking through the restaurant, you look about to see whether someone (especially someone in your section) is trying to catch your eye.

If a table is waiting for overdue food (due perhaps to the kitchen being overwhelmed), do not hide from them. Instead, keep them apprised of the situation. If your manager permits, offer them something to keep them happy and occupied as they wait, such as a green salad or cup of soup.

**REMAINING YOUR CUSTOMERS'
KEY POINT OF CONTACT**

If you work in a restaurant that has assistant servers, food runners, table bussers, liquor runners, and who knows what else, most of the staff's visits to your tables will be by someone other than you. As a result, your customers may hardly know that you are their waiter, and they are unlikely to tip you well given the lack of personal connection. To avoid this, try to take over some of the delivery duties, whether of food or liquor, and make the extra visit to make sure that everything is to their liking. In so doing, you can maintain your standing as the key server. This is particularly important if you keep your own tips (rather than pooling them) and if you wish to create a group of satisfied, regular customers.

CELEBRATIONS

If you notice that a group of your diners is celebrating something, whether that means ordering champagne or opening a gift, ask politely whether this is a special day for them. If it is, ask your manager if you can give them free wine, or ask the kitchen to make something special for them, such as an unusual dessert. Volunteer to take a picture of them to mark the occasion.

When you see someone taking a picture of her group of diners, volunteer to do so so that the entire party can be in the picture. And when you give them the check later on, preface this with a comment such as, "I trust the picture will come out well." Re-connecting with them in this personal way at the end of the meal can have them thinking favorably of you when it comes time to leave a tip.

EFFICIENCY

There are many ways for a server to become more efficient. For example:

- Learn the best way to organize trays.

- Use both hands—if you make a trip with only one

hand full, you have cut in half the amount of service you are offering on that trip.

- Do not leave a table without having asked your guests whether there is anything else you can get or do for them.

- If you see that your diners have nearly finished their coffee (or iced tea or soda), rather than approaching their table and asking whether they would like more coffee, bring the coffee pot along and then ask them.

In general, learn to anticipate your customers' needs. If someone orders something messy, like ribs or lobster, bring extra napkins. As you gain experience, you will know that anyone ordering a steak in your restaurant will appreciate having a steak knife, of course, but he may also want steak sauce, just as someone ordering lamb may appreciate mint sauce. If you notice that British diners like to have malt vinegar with their French fries, bring it automatically rather than waiting to be asked for it.

POLITENESS

When communicating with your guests, use an appropriate volume and tone of voice. If your voice is too soft, you will sound nervous and may frustrate your customers. This is most likely to be a problem in a noisy restaurant or if your customers are elderly and hard of hearing. A more typical problem is speaking too loudly, which makes you seem aggressive and uncultured.

Do not eat or drink in view of the guests. Do not have personal conversations—let alone arguments—with other waiters within your customers' earshot.

Other Important Don'ts:

- Talk across a customer's table. This is rude. It also means you may be spitting on their food.

- Touch the food or the eating surface of the dishes.

- Refill drinks over the table. Instead of taking the chance of spilling coffee, water, or iced tea on customers or their phones, remove the glass or cup and refill it next to the table.

- Reach across one customer to serve another. In addition to being rude and extremely annoying, it also risks knocking something into the offended customer's lap.

- Take sides regarding who gets the bill. When two or more customers argue over the tab, do not get involved. Instead, simply place the check in the middle of the table and let them settle it among themselves.

- Pester your guests. If you ask them how they are doing every time you pass by, you will annoy them. After you have checked in a moment or two after they receive their order, you do not need to ask them anything until they are (nearly) finished with that course. Instead, just pass by the table and stay alert to whether anyone is signaling that he wants something. If you make eye contact with a diner who does not want anything, just smile and keep working.

- Ask, "Do you need change?" when a guest pays in cash. Doing so makes it sound like you are accusing him of being so poor that he needs every penny or that you expect to receive the balance due as a tip. Instead, simply say that you'll return with the change immediately. When there is no need for change, your guest will tell you.

- Use off-color language or swear words, or make sexist or racist comments.

TEAMWORK

Even in an establishment where you are allowed to keep your own tips, try your best to help your fellow servers—but only when your own section is perfectly under control. If another server is in the weeds, get water or take orders for him. You will develop a great deal of goodwill with him and with your manager.

TEAMING UP WITH ANOTHER WAITER

Team up with a waiter in an adjoining section. When necessary, help clean and bus his tables, run his food, refill drinks and so on—in exchange for him doing the same for you. This will improve your service and efficiency, and largely eliminate your being "in the weeds" (completely overwhelmed) when you get an extremely large group of guests.

It may be your busser's job to refill water glasses and replenish the roll basket, but if he is failing to do so, then you should step up to the plate. If your guests have to look for you when they want a refill, you are falling down in your responsibilities.

MENU KNOWLEDGE

The more knowledgeable you are about the menu, the more diners will consider you a good waiter:

- Know the recipes used for all specialty drinks. (For more about serving beer, wine, and liquor, see Chapter 5, p. 149.)

- Know how to help people meet their specific dietary requirements. For example, take the time to learn what menu items would be most appropriate for:

  - Vegetarians; vegans

  - Diabetics

  - Those avoiding carbohydrates or abundant calories

  - Those allergic to eggs, wheat (gluten), or shellfish

- The lactose intolerant (no milk or dairy)

- Should your restaurant run out of something on the menu, or offer a dish with an ingredient that your guest wants to avoid, know what you can offer in place of it. For instance, maybe you are out of the chicken and leek pie, but the chicken and leek risotto is still available.

You should know everything on your menu—wine, appetizers, entrées, desserts, and so on. You need to know whether the shrimp is fresh or frozen, the broccoli local or not, the oranges from Florida or California, whether there is sugar in the salsa, what is in the meatballs, what is in the crab cakes besides crab, whether the salmon is wild or farmed. If the asparagus soup has cream in it, can it be made without the cream (or is it pre-mixed at the beginning of the shift and thus no changes are possible)? How many wings are in an order? What sort of oil is used to fry the chicken?

Doing your homework on the menu is important for other reasons as well. For example, when you consistently need to ask someone else, such as the manager or bartender, about an item, it harms you in two ways. It slows down the service for the guest and takes your time, and it lessens the guest's regard for you. Both of these factors may affect your tip. Moreover, your lack of knowledge about the menu lessens your ability to up-sell pricier dishes.

It helps if you have tasted everything on the menu. But whether you drink alcohol or not, eat red meat or not, you need to be able to describe any food and drinks your restaurant offers. It is no excuse to say, "I'm sorry, I don't drink." If you can't describe what you are serving, you should not be serving it.

Know which items are particularly tasty and a particularly good value. This is especially important for appetizers, because you will often be encouraging people to buy appetizers they had not intended to purchase, so if they are pleased with these appetizers they will form a very good opinion of you and your suggestions.

EXAMPLE: SELLING THE FOOD

Learn to give guests a complete—and winning—description of each menu item. Consider this descriptive picture of a cheeseburger:

Ingredients (including the weight of the main protein): "Our cheeseburger is six ounces of beef topped with melted cheese—either Swiss or American. It's available with grilled onions or mushrooms, or as a bacon burger—with melted cheese and three tasty bacon slices on top."

Preparation: "The beef is grilled over charcoal. Our chef normally serves it medium rare—seared on the outside yet still pink and juicy on the inside—but of course you can have it cooked however you like."

How it is served: "The cheeseburger is served either on a traditional bun or focaccia bread. It comes with French fries or onion rings."

Extras: "Many of our guests like to add a big salad to go with it, whether a garden salad, a Caesar salad, or a tomato and onion salad."

More extras: "Would you like a draft beer with it? Maybe a glass of a luscious red wine?"

Time to table: Explain how long it will take to prepare the item, particularly if it will be more than 10-12 minutes. (If the table will be ordering appetizers, this may not matter, because you will presumably place the order with the kitchen well before they have finished their appetizers, thus eliminating the need to wait for this item.)

The price of the item, and the price of any extra items. "Our cheeseburger is $9.95. If you'd like to add one of those salads, the combination is just $12.95."

Noteworthy aspects: "The salads are normally $5.95, so you get a great deal if you add a salad to your cheeseburger order."

Know Your Restaurant and Town

Know whether your restaurant is mentioned in prominent blogs, guides, and the like—and what they say about it. And if you are lucky enough to work at a restaurant with an interesting history, you can get a great deal of mileage out of a good story about the owner, the architect, the local area, and so on. For instance, if you work at a place that was frequented by Al Capone and his lieutenants in the 1920s, you can relate this along with whatever details are of interest to new diners. If local lore has it that he loved the pasta there, all the better.

Many diners will want to know about other businesses and sights near your restaurant. You can help them if you know whether the nearby museum is within walking distance, which bar offers the best Irish music, the nearest drug store open late, and so on. Similarly, be ready to talk about local events, including whatever of note happened earlier that day.

Learn the history of the neighborhood. "A century ago, this was the jewelry district, but the only remaining traces of that are the two jeweler's shops in the arcade across the street."

When Guests Are Finished

How do you know when a guest is finished? Guests can signal this by placing the knife and fork together on the plate, putting their napkins on the table, or pushing their plates away from themselves. If possible, wait until all of your guests have finished their meals before clearing the plates. This is not only common courtesy, but also keeps the slowest eater at your table from feeling awkward or uncomfortable. (Of course, if a guest insists upon having his or her plates removed, do so. A guest's preferences overrule the standard procedure.)

After your guests have ordered as much as they are likely to, have their checks printed and ready to be given to them whenever they request it. Give the check to the person who asked for it. If it is unclear who is to be given the check, put it in the middle of the table.

Guests may linger for the longest time, but when they are ready to leave they're often in an all-fired hurry. Be ready to give guests the bill once they have ordered (or declined) dessert and coffee. And once you have given it, judge whether they want to pay immediately and, if so, accept their payment and give them change as quickly as you can. This is when they are deciding what to tip you, so ultra-prompt service at this stage is extremely important for you.

Rather than asking whether a guest needs change, say, "I'll be right back with the change" and then return with it. Do not take the tip from the table until the party has left. If you happen to see the tip, say, "Thank you very much," no matter whether it is large or small.

If your restaurant has a car valet service, ask your customers whether they have valeted their cars when you present the bill. If so, offer to give any tickets to the valet attendant outside so that the cars will be waiting for them when they leave.

Boxing food. If your customers want to take their leftovers home in a doggy bag (or these days, a box), do the boxing for them. Not only do few customers want to box their own meals, but you can do so with less risk of spillage. Separate different items—if necessary, put them in separate boxes. Then write the date and the name of the food on the boxes, so that your customers can glance at them in the refrigerator later on and remember what they brought home (and figure out whether the food is still safe to eat).

SAYING GOODBYE

The moments guests remember most are their first and last impressions of a restaurant. Just as you put extra effort into greeting them and making them feel welcome when they arrived, leave them with a sincere goodbye. Thank them for coming and for the opportunity to serve them. For example, "It was a pleasure to take care of you today. I hope you'll come again soon. I'll be very pleased to take care of you again."

Showing real gratitude for their business will increase the odds that they will return. You can also mention anything unusual you might have done for your guests, but do so in an unassuming way. For instance, "I'm glad we had the type of hot dog your son prefers." Try to perform one or more small courtesies as your guests depart. Help someone out of his chair, put on her coat, or retrieve packages. If it is raining and you are not busy, offer to escort your guest to her car with an umbrella.

CONCLUSION

You will not get—or deserve—a large tip simply because you did one or two things well for a table. The entire dining experience should be excellent.

Appendix:
Reading The Table

There is great value in being able to "read a table." Reading a table is knowing without even asking what sort of food, drink, and service a group of customers will want. In time, you will learn how to interpret a group's mood with relative ease. Once you can read a group and tailor your service to their needs, you can boost your tips and establish a substantial group of regulars.

Learn how to anticipate what a guest wants by paying close attention to what the guest is wearing, her body carriage, overall energy level, tone of voice, the packages she is carrying, and so on. You can generally sense in no time whether she is in a hurry or hoping to relax, worried or celebrating. The more attuned you are to your guests, the more easily you can serve them in the way they will most value.

Guests give off hints as to what they value and what mood they are in:

- You may learn from the way someone is dressed what they value—someone dressed nattily versus someone dressed casually may value something fancy and traditional rather than something inexpensive.

- Notice how a guest speaks. Their tone of voice and facial expressions, along with the words they use, reveal a lot. For instance, someone may be skeptical about whether the fish special features fresh fish on a Monday—so when they say, "Really? It's fresh, is it?" their tone of voice may indicate their skepticism rather than their acceptance. Paying attention to such subtleties can clue you in as to how best to communicate with a particular guest.

- Sometimes there will be little guess work involved. If the guests are older women discussing diets, for example, consider mentioning low-calorie items such as the fresh vegetables or dinner salads.

Handling Problems
Addressing Mistakes

Everyone makes mistakes, including great waiters. They forget to order the steak rare instead of medium rare, bring a drink to a table of teetotalers, or drop a plate filled with pasta. Whatever the error, it's the reaction to it that is likely to be more important than the actual mistake. For example, after the pasta tumbles to the ground, if you (and those around you) rush about in a mad panic, you will upset the guests more than the original dropping of the plate. The best way to handle this is to apologize sincerely but briefly, and then clear up the mess—or have the busser do so—quickly and without any fuss.

In a busy restaurant, you will inevitably make mistakes, probably on most of your shifts. When you handle your mistakes properly and without needing management to get involved, you increase your chances for a good tip. Depending upon the restaurant, the particular manager, and your relationship with her, the extent to which managers get involved in problems may vary greatly. Some managers tend to be very hands-off, whereas others are over-involved. Some managers want to know if even the tiniest thing goes wrong at a table; others can't be bothered to help even when you ask.

We suggest you handle your own mistakes as much as possible, regardless of the type of manager you have. If your manager needs to fix one of your mistakes (forgetting to ring in diners' beers, for example) and gives your table a free dessert, you may get a couple extra dollars in your tip. However, your manager will remember that she had to intervene and write you up for the mistake. Should this happen multiple times, your shifts may be reduced or changed.

Most guests just want their grievances to be heard, so simply admitting your mistakes and promptly fixing them is usually enough to satisfy them. So, in most instances, you shouldn't need your manager's help at all. On the other hand, if the mistake is not yours—a kitchen error, a misquoted wait time for a table—feel free to inform management. Doing so may make it possible to get free appetizers or desserts for your table without you suffering any harmful repercussions.

CUSTOMER COMPLAINTS

Sensible complaints from guests can provide a restaurant with valuable information with which it can improve its performance. Handled in a manner that makes a guest feel that he has been heard fully and his complaint taken seriously, properly-addressed complaints can convert an unhappy guest into a devoted customer, and forestall his broadcasting his complaint or ill feelings to the world.

Some guidelines for handling complaints:

- Before acting or re-acting, listen carefully and make sure you understand a guest's complaint or problem fully. Bear in mind that many guests just want to be heard, so listening well may be enough to satisfy them.

- Restate the problem briefly, thereby showing that you understand it. Ask the guest to agree that you have restated the problem correctly.

- Express regret for what occurred in a sincere manner.

- Agree with some part of the complaint, if possible. ("I agree— you should have gotten your drinks sooner.")

- Know what you can do to rectify the problem without having to get a manager's approval. This may mean taking something off the bill or giving a free appetizer, dessert, or drink. Or it may involve promising to pay for a guest's clothing to be cleaned or replaced.

- Handle the complaint immediately—either by yourself or, if that is not possible, by getting your manager involved.

- If the restaurant is at fault, apologize, and note that all steps will be taken to prevent a recurrence. Be sure your apology is sincere; an empty apology is likely to annoy rather than pacify your guest.

· Thank the guest for making the complaint. "Thank you for bringing this to our attention. We'll do all we can to make sure nothing of this sort happens again."

You may be limited in terms of what you can offer your guest to make up for whatever went wrong. In that case, the phrase, "What I can do is..." shows you want to help your guests—at least up to the limits of your authority.

WHEN TO GET YOUR MANAGER INVOLVED

Although it is generally a good idea to handle your section without relying on managerial assistance, there are some circumstances in which managerial involvement is called for.

For example, customers may make requests that you are unable to meet, perhaps because they are contrary to restaurant policy or because they are simply too time-consuming or expensive to be warranted. For example, your restaurant may have a policy that no group's bill can be split more than four ways and you have a group of twelve that wants it split twelve ways—with different amounts for each person. If, after telling your customers that this is against restaurant policy, they may argue that they have the right to do this. Instead of arguing with them, tell them that you understand and will get the manager for them—with the understanding that if she okays this, you will be happy to do as they wish. The manager will probably deny them the "right" to do this, but your customers will still appreciate you as being on their side—and tip you well as a result.

Do not let yourself be drawn into arguments with difficult customers. Instead, involve your manager as quickly as you can.

HANDLING ABSURD COMPLAINTS

You will probably get all sorts of absurd complaints:
- I ordered my hamburger medium rare, not reddish-pink.
- The broccoli is too green and the lobster is too red.
- The steak tartar is not cooked.
- The color of the plate does not provide enough contrast with the entrée to be Instagram-worthy.

Don't laugh at your guest's ignorance or foolishness. If you can solve the problem easily by having the item cooked longer or a sauce added, do so. If you are at a loss for how to solve it, get your manager involved.

WHEN CUSTOMERS FAIL TO PAY

There are two relatively common non-payment issues. The first occurs when a customer is unable to pay for his meal. Most restaurants will have a set procedure for handling this, but it will be up to your manager, not you, to deal with this. A second and more common problem is a guest walking out without paying—either due to forgetfulness or a desire to avoid paying. If you see a guest is in the process of leaving without yet having paid the bill, politely and tactfully remind him of the bill. It is quite possible that he simply overlooked the fact that he had not yet paid. If he continues to leave, or if he has already left, don't chase after him and try to drag him back to the restaurant. Instead, immediately notify your manager of what has happened.

RUDE BEHAVIOR

Inevitably, you will have rude customers. Guests often arrive hungry and tired, perhaps stressed from a difficult day at work or a long day shopping or minding their kids. Their irritability may result in ill-mannered treatment of anyone they encounter. As a server, try your best not to take their rudeness to heart. Instead, serve them well and professionally and chalk their rudeness up to their situation, not your behavior.

MANAGERS' AND SERVERS' ADVICE TO AVOID DRAMA

"Make yourself easy to work with. If you get along with your co-workers you are easier to manage and thus a more desirable employee."

Upscale casual restaurant manager

"When they're working, they need to put their personal life aside. No one needs to hear that they've broken up with their boyfriend."

Fine dining restaurant owner

"Don't assume customers give a s--- about your personal problems."

Gastropub owner

"Don't listen to what your colleagues say when they're having a bad day. Think about your happy place and about helping people, which is what you're here for."

Airport restaurant server

"Leave your personal stuff at the door. Remember you are here for your money, not to get wrapped up in drama."

Upscale casual restaurant server

"Smile a lot. Say, 'It's not a problem' in response to whatever occurs."

Pub restaurant server

"The key is patience, with both colleagues and guests."

Fine dining restaurant server

Taking Care of Your Health

Waiting tables is demanding work. If you work more than a shift or two each week, you are likely to experience aches and pains in your feet, knees, back, and elsewhere in your body. There is a lot you can do to reduce wear and tear on your body:

- Wear comfortable shoes, with good arch support and cushioning. This will reduce the impact on your feet, knees, and back.

- If you alternate two different pairs of shoes, not only will they last longer, but your feet will also benefit from not always wearing the exact same shoes. Your feet won't get as tired and you will be less prone to develop athlete's foot.

- Stand tall—good posture will help you avoid later back and shoulder issues.

- Stretch before and after work, even if only briefly.

- Moisturize your hands if they are often in water.

- Strengthen your quadriceps, back, shoulder, arm, and wrist muscles to facilitate the demands of carrying heavy trays. Pay particular attention to your core— your stomach, lower back, and related areas.

- Avoid the drug and booze scene typical of many restaurants' wait staffs.

Safety

Wear non-slip shoes if possible. They will allow you to move more surely in the kitchen and bar areas, where the floor may be wet or greasy.

When lifting anything heavy, try to keep your back straight and "lift with your knees."

Anxiety, Stress, and Depression

Many servers are unable to leave the job behind when they are off duty—they remember the annoying diners, pushy managers, and the impossible pressure to perform perfectly. The ability to relax and get away from the job—mentally as well as physically—is important. Strenuous exercise, meditation, and yoga are all good antidotes to anxiety and stress. These and other techniques designed to keep you healthy are preferable to resorting to drugs, alcohol, and the like.

Drugs and Alcohol

Many restaurants and bars have a server culture that encourages after-work—or even before or during work—consumption of alcohol and/or drugs (especially marijuana and cocaine). We certainly know of restaurants in the Bay Area, for example, at which most of the staff are regular pot smokers. And with the loosening of drug laws in various states, we assume that drug consumption is likely to increase.

If you don't want to be surrounded by drinkers, weed smokers, or coke users, by all means avoid establishments that are rife with them. If you are an abstainer or occasional consumer and end up working in a restaurant with an alcohol or drug culture, though, we caution you that you may find yourself influenced to consume—and may wake up to find that you are not an abstainer or merely occasional consumer anymore.

Beer, Hard Liquor, and Wine

Chapter Five

Introduction

One of the keys to making good money waiting tables is to work in a restaurant that serves a substantial amount of wine and liquor, preferably expensive wine and liquor. Expensive drinks increase the tab, which in turn usually increases a server's tip. In some cases, restaurants will hire servers without a substantial knowledge of wine and alcoholic beverages. However, the more a restaurant depends upon the sale of pricey wine, for instance, the more it is likely to require that prospective servers possess considerable knowledge. And at some establishments, such as upscale wine bars, a sophisticated knowledge of wine is an absolute requirement. There are some interesting exceptions, however. In restaurants with sommeliers, servers may be expected to involve a sommelier in a table's choice of wine, thereby lessening the need for the servers themselves to be knowledgeable.

Although the above discussion focuses on wine, much the same could be said of beer. Given the advent of a sophisticated beer culture in the country, many restaurants now expect waiters to be knowledgeable about craft and foreign beers.

Knowing a good deal about wine, beer, and hard liquor will not just make you eligible to work at restaurants requiring such knowledge, however. You will also profit by providing a better service to guests and, in many cases, by managing to convincingly pitch a fancier than house bottle of wine, you will get a substantially larger tip.

Beer

Serving beer is not particularly complicated: there is not a great deal to know about pouring beer from a bottle into a glass (except to tilt the glass). However, many restaurants and bars now offer a dizzying array of beers, and customers expect servers to be able to describe them in some detail.

Beer Descriptions

Customers are likely to know the mass-brews, such as Budweiser and Heineken, but not all of the other offerings a restaurant may feature, such as local, regional, and distant-origin craft beers. As a server, you will want to be ready to describe them in some detail, including type (India pale ale, wheat beer, etc.), alcohol percentage, hoppiness, and so on. If your restaurant attracts "hopsters," know what type of hops the craft beers use.

The standard descriptions include:

- *IPAs (India pale ales) and pales ales:* refreshing, crisp, hoppy, floral, citrus (and even dank).

- *Stouts and porters:* rich, smooth, malty, caramel, coffee, chocolate, milky.

- *Ambers and browns:* malty, balanced, smooth, semi-sweet, caramel.

- *Pilsners and lagers:* crisp, light, balanced, refreshing, drinkable. Because these beers are often enjoyed at particularly cold temperatures, serving them in a "frosted glass" may be considered a plus.

For those looking to drink a great deal of beer, "session strength" describes a beer comparatively low in alcohol and therefore one that can be consumed in quantity.

MATCHING BEER AND FOOD

Many restaurants and pubs now emphasize matching beer (rather than wine) with food. If you work in this sort of establishment, you will want to know the beers on offer well enough to help guests match their food with the appropriate brews.

WHEN TO SUGGEST A PITCHER

When two or more customers in a group order draft beer, consider suggesting that they order a pitcher (assuming your restaurant offers them). Not only will this encourage your guests to drink more, but it will also limit your work because you'll only need to worry about bringing a pitcher to the table occasionally rather than individual beers whenever one guest runs dry. You also won't burden your bartender with a long stream of requests for beers to be poured.

Additional Resources

Julia Herz and Gwen Conley, *Beer Pairing*
Marty Nachel, *Beer for Dummies*
Randy Mosher, *Tasting Beer: An Insider's Guide to the World's Greatest Drink*
Jeff Alworth, *The Beer Bible*

Certification for Beer Servers

Cicerone Certified Beer Server. A set of four exams that require substantial knowledge of beer storage, service, styles (modern and historical), ingredients, brewing processes, and food pairings, along with an ability to distinguish different beers and flavors. The first exam, which is not particularly difficult, is currently priced at $69. The succeeding exams are both more difficult and pricier—$395, $795, and $995, respectively. In addition to the time and effort required to pass the advanced exams, a typical candidate would need to spend a substantial amount on books and other study materials (ugh) as well as beer (yum).

Only would-be beer specialists and true devotees are likely to profit from tackling all four of these exams. On the other hand, those who wish merely to demonstrate a reasonable amount of knowledge of and interest in beer might profit from passing the first exam. Being able to cite this level of mastery and interest could certainly help you get a job at a beer-oriented restaurant (or bar), and the knowledge and skill developed would help you perform your job well.

HARD LIQUOR

BASICS

As a server, it's critical to learn the commonly ordered drinks, and what you need to know to complete a drink order. For a martini, for instance, you need to know whether it is to be gin or vodka, dry or sweet (normal ratios of vermouth to gin have evolved over time; generations ago, the usual ratio was a sweet 3:1 or 4:1, but now the ratio is likely to be a dry 6:1 or 8:1 or even 10:1), and your guest's preferred garnish (onions—which actually turn a martini into a Gibson, olives, a twist of lemon, or some combination).

SELLING MORE

If a customer has nearly finished a drink, shortly before the appetizer or main course will be served, ask, "Your appetizer/entrée will come out in just a moment. Would you like to have another glass (or drink) so that you can enjoy it with your meal?"

LANGUAGE MATTERS

The way you phrase your interactions with diners matters. For example, if you ask someone, "Did you need another drink?" or "You don't want another drink, do you?" the guest cannot answer yes without sounding like a drunkard.

The chances of a positive answer increase with positive phrasing of the question: "How about another drink?" Or, better yet, "Shall I freshen your drink?" Or, "Can I top that up for you?" A guest can answer positively to these invitations without sounding like he's a problem drinker.

Try to avoid having to ask, "What were you drinking?" This shows that you do not remember a guest's order and need to be reminded of it when she asks for another glass.

Up-Selling

The better you know your beverage menu and stock, the better you'll be able to up-sell. Many drinks can be served with the house liquor—the cheapest version of that type of liquor that the restaurant stocks—or with a fancier, more expensive liquor. For instance, any drink with gin in it can be served with cheap gin or a "call" brand— something your guest requests by name. If a guest orders a gin martini, for example, you can ask whether he would prefer Tanqueray, Beefeater, or Sipsmith, or just the house pour.

The same is true for liquors served straight. For example, if someone orders a scotch—especially if she orders it "neat" or "up," which suggests she is particular about the taste given that she is not adulterating it with soda—you can ask her whether she would like Macallan, Ardbeg, Highland Park, or whatever other single malt your establishment stocks, rather than the house blend. If she does indeed order a single malt rather than the "house" or "well" liquor, she will probably be paying two or three times as much. If you have five customers a shift ordering two brand name rather than house liquors, you will make about $15 extra in tips each shift. Assuming you work 250 shifts a year, that is $3,750 in additional tip income!

If you work at a reasonably fancy restaurant, know at least three "call" brands for the liquors that are most popular with your guests, whether those are scotch, Irish whiskey, vodka, gin, rum, tequila, brandy, bourbon, or rye. For instance, if you have many requests for scotch, you should know several single malts from each of the key regions: Islay, the Highlands, and perhaps even Speyside. And you should know which brands are peatiest (Ardbeg, Lagavulin, and Laphroaig from Islay, as it happens), which are smoothest, and so on.

After-Dinner Drinks

After-dinner drinks are a special category. Most are relatively expensive (think cognac, port, dessert wines, and the like), so you can make large tips if your guests order them. Therefore, before asking whether guests want coffee, which signals the end of the meal, inquire about after-dinner drinks first.

UP-SELLING NON-ALCOHOLIC DRINKS

Liquor isn't the only beverage that can be up-sold. Espressos, cappuccinos, and lattés are more expensive than plain coffee. The same may also be true in your restaurant of fancy teas.

YOUR OWN CONSUMPTION

Drinking on the job is obviously unprofessional. At some restaurants, it is tolerated—and many servers may indeed drink together or with customers. At other restaurants, drinking on the job is a firing offense for which there is zero tolerance.

If colleagues or customers want you to join them in drinking and you wish to avoid doing so, you can simply say, "No thank you, not when I'm working."

LIQUOR LINGO

- *Back (or chaser):* the companion drink, in a second glass, to accompany the primary drink. Someone ordering whiskey may order "water, back," meaning that he wants a glass of water in addition to the whiskey. Or he might ask for a beer chaser for his whiskey.

- *Call liquor:* any liquor other than "house" or "well" liquor. The term refers to "calling" the liquor by brand name (Tanqueray or Beefeater) rather than simply saying "gin and tonic."

- *Dirty:* with a splash of olive juice.

- *Dry:* little or no vermouth—usually referring to martinis.

- *House pour:* also called a "well" drink. The liquor served when a guest does not specify a brand preference. Almost always inexpensive brands.

- *Muddled:* mixed together, usually referring to mint or other item partially crushed to derive its flavors.

- *Neat:* alcohol drink served without ice or mixer.

- *On the rocks:* drink served over ice cubes or ice shavings.

- *Proof:* refers to the percent of alcohol in a beverage, derived from a scale in which 200 is equal to 100 percent alcohol. To arrive at the percent alcohol, divide the proof number by 2. Thus a whiskey which is 80 proof is actually 40 percent alcohol.

- *Rimmed:* salt or sugar around the rim.

- *Shot* (or *jigger*): a measure of liquor, usually between 1 and 1 ½ ounces.

- *Straight up* (often abbreviated as *"up"*): a drink served without ice or mixer.

- *Top shelf:* expensive liquor brands, often stored on the top shelf behind the bar.

- *Virgin:* without alcohol.

- *Well drink:* standard or "house" brand of liquor.

- *With a twist:* drink served with a twist of lemon (or lime).

Additional Resources

Perry Luntz, *Whiskey & Spirits for Dummies*

Anthony Dias Blue, *The Complete Book of Spirits*

Lew Bryson, *Tasting Whiskey: An Insider's Guide to the Unique Pleasures of the World's Finest Spirits*

Jim Murray, *Jim Murray's Whiskey Bible*

Dominic Roskrow, *Michael Jackson's Complete Guide to Single Malt Scotch*

Dave Broom, *Gin: The Manual*

Dave Broom, *Rum: The Manual*

Michael Gibson, *The Sommelier Prep Course: An Introduction to the Wine, Beers, and Spirits of the World*

Ray Foley, *Bartending for Dummies*

WINE

GETTING STARTED

Serving wine can be the trickiest—but also the most lucrative—part of your job. If you know little about wine when you start working at your restaurant, at the very least learn something about a handful of the most popular wines your restaurant serves. Over the course of your first two weeks, work up to half a dozen whites and a dozen reds. At the same time, learn what sort of wine best matches different types of food. If yours is an Italian restaurant, for instance, learn what best matches the main pasta types (which is generally a matter of the type of sauce used—tomato versus cream-based, for instance), the different veal dishes, and so on. You can probably sort the entrees into fewer than a dozen groups in terms of wine pairings.

Before you start each shift, look at your notes on the characteristics of the key wines and the best pairings of wine and food.

As time goes on, you'll be able to guide guests with greater assurance as you learn the nuances of both the food and the wine. For example, if someone wants a wine to accompany a rabbit and chorizo jambalaya, you will know to mention a couple of zinfandels that have the fruit and strong flavor to stand up to the jambalaya's massive flavors.

Help for the overwhelmed guest. After you have taken the food order, take the wine order. If your guests seem overwhelmed by the choice of wines, consider suggesting something. It can also be very helpful to give guests an overview of their options. For instance, you can show the guest the wine menu and note where she will find wines by the glass, wines by the half-bottle, and wines by the bottle— or wines by country and region or grape varietal.

MORE DIFFICULT CHALLENGES

If you have to match several entrees that are very different in taste and would ordinarily require very different wines, you have two

options. The more sophisticated approach is to aim for som
between—and mention what you would have recommended ⌐.
entrée on its own. This will demonstrate your knowledge and also give
your guests the chance to choose to match only one or two of the
entrées. For example, a guest who has ordered a delicate fish entrée
that would ordinarily pair with an expensive white wine might prefer
to have the wine match the steak her partner ordered because it's his
birthday—or because she prefers red wine anyway.

A simpler approach is to ask the guest who is in charge of ordering
whether she prefers red or white wines. Then ask whether she prefers
dry, medium, or sweet wines. With this information in hand, you can
suggest three wines of the appropriate color and dryness, each at a
different price level. (If the guest has a country preference, then you
can further focus your suggestions.)

Be leery of suggesting pricey wines to guests unless you know
their tastes or are helping them match a very expensive entrée. By
suggesting low or mid-priced wines you will give them confidence
that you are not trying to bilk them.

WINE RULES

Matching the color of the wine with the color of the food is a simple
rule to begin with. White wines are generally lighter in flavor than red
wines and therefore match well with mild favors, such as fish, fowl, and
other white dishes. Red wines, being heavier, match well with stronger
favors, such as red meat and foods with heavy or spicy sauces.

Bear in mind that there are plenty of exceptions to this "rule."
Exceptions regarding the wine: some white wines, such as New Zealand
sauvignon blancs and French burgundies, may be stronger than some
red wines, including many pinot noirs. Exceptions regarding the food:
consider the preparation of the food, not just the main ingredient. Despite
being a red meat, veal when prepared simply or with a light sauce may
benefit from pairing with a white wine. On the other hand, veal parmigiana,
with cheese and a rich tomato sauce, begs for a strong red wine.

If a table will have different wines, the order in which they are served
is important. The first wines should not spoil the palate and thereby ruin
the taste of the wines that follow. Thus, the suggestions for wine order:

- Dry before sweet • Light before full-bodied
- White before red • Middling before great
- Young before old • Table wines (10—15% alcohol) before fortified wines (20—30%)

Some guests will mention wines that they like and ask for something similar to one or another of them. In this case, you will need to know enough about wine in general, as well as the wines your restaurant serves, in order to compare wines you suggest to those she is familiar with. This may, of course, require the help of your sommelier or manager.

You will benefit in multiple ways from your knowledge of the wine menu. When you please guests with a good pairing of wine with their food, they'll be inclined to increase your tip. They will also be more likely to choose you as their waiter when they return to the restaurant—and to become regulars of yours. They will view you as a knowledgeable and professional waiter. And the more they like the wine, the more wine they'll order.

Serving a wine. Present the bottle to the guest who ordered it so she can make sure it is what she ordered—the same wine and vintage. Open the bottle, presenting the cork to that guest so that she can smell it and check to make sure the wine is not "skunked," and then pour a small amount of wine in her glass for a taste. Once she tastes it and approves, pour the wine for the other guests, and then fill the remainder of her glass. When pouring wine, do not let the bottle touch the rim of the glass. And remember to handle the glasses themselves only by their stem, not by their bowls.

When you pour the wine, twist the bottle a quarter turn as you complete the pouring. This will prevent drops running down the side of the bottle.

Serve relatively small portions of white wine because it is chilled; large portions would warm in the glass while waiting to be consumed. The bottle, in the meantime, should be kept in an ice bucket so that the wine is kept chilled. When serving it, use a towel to prevent the bottle's wetness from dripping onto the table or the guests.

OPENING WINE AT THE TABLE

Be sure you know how to open wine bottles at the table. Doing so reassures guests that the wine they ordered is the wine they are getting. If the bottle is already opened when it arrives at the table, they may worry that a cheaper wine was poured into the bottle back in the bar. If you need practice, come in before your shift and open the bottles the bartender wants opened for those wines she'll serve by the glass that shift.

Remove the wrapping around the bottle top and remove the cork without smearing your hands all over the spout. If you are opening a champagne bottle, do so quietly and without fuss rather than popping it.

Selling more wine. The easiest way to increase a table's bill is to sell a bottle of wine or, better yet, an additional bottle of wine. Start by assuming that a table will order wine. Ask, "Have you found the right wine to match your entrée?" And if the table has ordered wine at the beginning of the meal, shift your focus to selling a second bottle. Bear in mind that doing so is particularly easy if a table is nearing the end of the first bottle before they've even started on their entrées. Just before the main course arrives, pour the remainder of the bottle into people's glasses. This is the perfect time to ask the person who ordered the initial bottle, "Would you care to have another bottle to enjoy with your meal?" If he declines a bottle of wine, suggest a half-bottle or carafe of wine. Note that if the second bottle is of a different wine, you will need to replace the wine glasses.

As a server, you will have many opportunities to sell wine: in your initial welcome to the group, when you take the appetizer order (and when you bring the appetizers), when you take the entrée order, after you put in the entrée order, when you bring the entrees, and after dinner (port or champagne).

What if he sends the wine back? Relatively few bottles of wine actually go bad, but some customers will invariably send back the bottles they ordered. This is usually because it does not taste the way they had hoped. Find out what your restaurant's policy is for handling this. In tricky situations you will want to involve your manager.

Additional Resources

Edmund O. Lawler, *Lessons in Wine Service*

Robert J. Harrington, *Food & Wine Pairing: A Sensory Experience*

Ed McCarthy and Mary Ewing-Mulligan, *Wine for Dummies* (and note the separate volumes in this series devoted to California, French, and Italian wines)

Ophelie Newman, *Wine Isn't Rocket Science*

Karen MacNeil, *The Wine Bible*

John Szabo, *Pairing Food & Wine for Dummies*

Janet Fletcher, *Cheese & Wine: A Guide to Selecting, Pairing, and Enjoying*

Andrew Dornenburg and Karen Page, *What to Drink with What You Eat: The Definitive Guide to Pairing Food with Wine, Beer, Spirits, Coffee, Tea—Even Water*

Bianca Bosker, *Cork Dork: A Wine-Fueled Adventure Among the Obsessive Sommeliers, Big Bottle Hunters, and Rogue Scientists Who Taught Me to Live for Taste*

OVER-SERVED GUESTS

Alcohol often changes guests' behavior, sometimes for the better and sometimes for the worse. Alcohol makes some guests happy, so happy that they may tip you magnificently. Adam has had guests made happy by alcohol tip him 50 to 100 percent of their bill because he laughed at their silly jokes. Alcohol makes other guests argumentative or even violent. Even in fancy restaurants, over-served guests may attack other guests for little or no reason.

As a server, you need to make judgment calls regarding how much a guest has already imbibed and whether he needs to be cut off denied more alcohol. Guests who want more alcohol seldom react well to being denied drinks, so it's usually best to involve your manager in this process. And regardless of how collected guests who are drinking heavily may seem, keep an extra eye on them because their behavior may be hard to predict.

Appendix:
Minimum Age To Serve Alcohol

STATE/ MINIMUM AGE TO STATE/ MINIMUM AGE TO TERRITORY SERVE ALCOHOL TERRITORY SERVE ALCOHOL

State/ Territory	Minimum Age	State/ Territory	Minimum Age
Alabama	19	Nebraska	19
Alaska	21	Nevada	21
Arizona	19	New Hampshire	18
Arkansas	19	New Jersey	18
California	18	New Mexico	19
Colorado	18	New York	18
Connecticut	18	North Carolina	18
DC	18	North Dakota	19
Delaware	18	Ohio	19
Florida	18	Oklahoma	18
Georgia	18	Oregon	18
Hawaii	18	Pennsylvania	18
Idaho	19	Rhode Island	18
Illinois	18	South Carolina	18
Indiana	19	South Dakota	18
Iowa	18	Tennessee	18
Kansas	18	Texas	18
Kentucky	19	Utah	21
Louisiana	18	Vermont	18
Maine	17	Virginia	18
Maryland	18	Washington	18
Massachusetts	18	West Virginia	18
Michigan	18	Wisconsin	18
Minnesota	18	Wyoming	18
Mississippi	18	Puerto Rico	18
Missouri	18	US Virgin Islands	18
Montana	18		

Increasing Professionalism

Chapter Six

ORDER-TAKER VS. SALES PERSON

An *order-taker* considers customers an unfortunately necessary part of his rotten job. He limits his interaction with customers to an absolute minimum. If he is asked about a particular menu item, he says "It's good." Or, "I dunno, I've never eaten it myself." If he is asked about the draft beers available, he hands the customer the beer list, saying "They're all on here." If it appears that the customers are not completely ready to order, he tells them he'll come back when they are ready, instead of helping them to make decisions. He doesn't encourage the ordering of appetizers or desserts, because serving extra courses means more work on his part.

By simply processing customers rather than serving them, an order-taker develops few if any regulars. He feels plagued by cheap customers who tip him poorly. As a result, he works extra shifts to make the money he needs, all the while complaining about his miserable job.

A *sales person*, on the other hand, views her job as an opportunity to make a lot of money through her own initiative and knowledge. She greets her guests with true pleasure because she is in fact happy to see them. She knows the restaurant's offerings thoroughly, including the daily specials, and knows how to describe them appetizingly. She pays close attention to her guests' comments, appearance, and mood, and asks questions to learn more about what might interest them. In this manner, she thereby up-sells effortlessly—in a way calculated to please her guests because she recommends items that are very much to their taste. She stays alert while on the floor, noticing whenever a guest wants something. Her proactive approach extends to making sure she works very efficiently, always thinking ahead.

A sales person enjoys her interactions with her guests, enjoys pleasing them, and as a result of her initiative and skill ends up with a large roster of regular guests. Her average bill is much higher than her order-taking colleague, and her tip percentage is higher, too. She considers herself a skilled professional and takes pride in her job.

CONCLUSION

If you intend to work in an upscale restaurant, or to make the most of your job in a less-than-fancy environment, you need to be a sales person, not just a simple order-taker.

Professionalism

The more you think of yourself as a professional, the higher the standards you will set for yourself. Professionalism has a number of dimensions:

Appearance. You take pride in your appearance as well as your performance.

Demeanor. Kids cry, bussers drop plates, the kitchen over-cooks meat, and even you make mistakes. If you keep your cool, you will appear more professional than if you express your frustration.

Do not pout, act out, or put on a show when a table tips you badly. Remember that the law of averages will kick in and some other tables will make up for this.

Even under difficult circumstances, always maintain an upbeat and professional demeanor. You also invariably use polite and appropriate language.

Discretion. Guests should not hear you complaining about customers, other employees, the food, or anything else. Nor should they see or hear you arguing with fellow employees, let alone with other guests. When you are in view or within the hearing of guests, consider yourself "onstage." Only when you cannot be seen or heard by them are you offstage.

Do not bad-mouth a customer or colleague to one of your guests, even if the guest is a regular with whom you have a well-established relationship. It is likely to make the regular guest a bit uncomfortable— not knowing how to respond and wondering whether you would ever say something rude about her to another guest.

Leaving your troubles at home. You do not let your personal issues interfere with your professional behavior, whether that means interacting with guests and colleagues. Similarly, you minimize (or, preferably, eliminate) your cell phone use while on the job.

Reliability. You show up on time, ready to work, every shift. You do not beg off shifts unless you are deathly ill or facing an unavoidable situation of substantial difficulty.

Responsibility. You take responsibility for your actions, bad as well as good, rather than looking to blame others.

Self-development. You do your best to develop your skills—both technical and social. You actively seek constructive criticism and advice, and pay attention to what the best professionals do.

Gauging your Professionalism

One way to gauge your professionalism is to compare yourself with your colleagues and with waiters who serve you when you are a guest at another restaurant.

Engaging With Guests

Dining out, especially at upscale restaurants, has evolved from a mere dining experience to a form of entertainment. This means that many restaurants—and not just fancy ones—value servers who can engage with guests in a pleasing manner. At a minimum, servers are expected to make pleasant social small talk with guests. Better than that, however, is the ability to amuse the guests (one of the reasons actors often make good servers). (As Chapter 1 notes, many restaurants now hire servers more on the basis of personality than of experience.)

There are numerous benefits to connecting with your guests. Diners who enjoy chatting with you will seek you out. It's much easier, and more profitable, to serve regular customers than others. The more you connect with your guests, the more pleasant and satisfying your interactions will be—and the more satisfaction you will get from pleasing them with your service. And, of course, the better your connection with your guests, the less likely they will be to give you a hard time if something goes wrong.

It is less difficult to chat with diners than with other strangers because they expect you to approach them and start chatting. For some servers, however, this is still a daunting prospect. This is especially true for introverted and inexperienced servers, or those who are in a very different environment than they are used to. For instance, a Manhattanite newly working in a small Louisiana town may not intuitively know how to relate to diners she's serving.

NOT ALL DINERS WANT TO CHAT

Although this section is devoted to helping you engage with guests, a key lesson is that not all diners want to chat with their waiters. Discerning which guests would like to chat among themselves or read quietly is critical. Finding the right balance between too much and too little interaction with your guests is a key skill to cultivate.

If you are uncomfortable or unsuccessful in chatting with diners, consult the rest of this chapter's suggestions for developing the necessary skills. Our advice focuses on developing basic chatting skills rather the ability to dazzle, on the principle that you need to learn to walk before you can run. Once you can walk, you can work on developing the ability to dazzle.

WHY DO SO MANY ACTORS WORK AS SERVERS?

Many people assume that actors often work as waiters because they need work they can easily ditch when offered a tryout for a part. There is some truth to this assumption, but it is only part of the explanation. Another reason is that serving is similar to acting. If you are happy to put on a performance for customers, then you will naturally fulfill one of a server's functions.

Actors bring a useful set of attitudes and behaviors to the job of waiting tables:

- They are prepared to forget about their own issues and act the part of someone putting on a show.
- They expect to smile and entertain people no matter how they are feeling themselves.
- Each day is a new performance—a chance to charm a new audience.

As Adam remarks: "Every table seems like an audience. You have a group of people sitting, listening to you with interest. And all you have to do is make food sound delicious and sell them on an experience. I get stage fright when greeting my first table every day. This is because I am still me, Adam, and I have yet to sink into my character, that of the server."

More than a few performers have gotten their "big break" from serving someone in the entertainment industry who liked their professionalism and engaging personality. They have profited from doing their job well and energetically.

PRACTICE

Don't be concerned if you currently lack the ability to engage strangers in conversation. You will have plenty of opportunity to develop your skills in public encounters that are a normal part of your day. You can practice on the people you encounter each day—the person who prints your business cards; the grocery checkout clerk;

local shop owners; etc. Taxi and Uber and Lyft drivers are perfect guinea pigs for you, too.

In practicing, look for the people who are probably most open to talking with you. Someone who smiles at you and turns toward you even slightly is a better target than someone who ignores you or frowns at you.

Don't feel that you need to say anything earth-shattering to open the conversation. Pleasant chit-chat is your aim—not setting the world to rights. The easiest way to start a conversation is to take advantage of one of three possible topics: the situation, your prospective conversation partner, yourself.

Further Tips

Bear in mind that your nonverbal communication will be at least as important as what you say. Look someone in the eye with a smile on your face and a twinkle in your eyes. Be relaxed, confident, and welcoming. Conveying that you are at ease puts others at ease.

If you have a sociable friend who successfully engages strangers in conversation, spend some time with him and observe how he does so. You will probably see that he is a good listener—something true of all good conversationalists—who enjoys asking questions to draw out the other person.

If you normally engage with your electronic devices instead of human beings, put your electronics away for large stretches of each day. Venture out with your cell phone turned off or simply leave it behind. Be open to the people you encounter along the way. If you are a commuter, it's relatively easy to connect with fellow commuters by talking about the late train or bus, asking about their reading material, and so on.

Extending the Conversation

If you are talking with someone who likes to talk, you will probably start getting some surplus information early on in your conversation. Nearly 40 percent of everyday speech consists of self-disclosure, such as telling people what we think or how we feel about something. For example, "This jacket? It's a Barbour. I spend a few months in London every year, so I like to have something that handles the English climate and looks appropriate to the Brits." You asked him about his jacket, but you now know he spends substantial time in London every year. You can take advantage of this surplus information by commenting on it or asking questions about it. "How do you manage that damp and windy climate of theirs?" Or, "What sort of business are you in that lets you hang out in London every year?" And so on. By taking advantage of the surplus information, you have the opportunity to drive the conversation in any number of different directions.

There are other types of surplus information available to you, too. In addition to what your conversation partner says, observe what she's wearing, how she's acting or reacting (shivering in the cold, for instance?), her expression, her physical features, what she's carrying, and so on.

Note, too, that you can influence the direction of the conversation toward topics that are of interest to you. This might be the classic cliché—"How 'bout them Mets?"—or whatever topics you are most knowledgeable about. So if you are a TV addict who knows everything about various Sci Fi series, see whether you can engage guests in a discussion about one of them—or, failing that, see whether you can entertain them with amusing comments about a recent episode.

FLIRTATION AND TIPS

Another form of engagement is flirting with customers. Although it may not be explicitly stated, cocktail waitresses in many establishments are expected to flirt with men. The same is true of waitresses in some restaurants—and not just Hooters, Twin Peaks, and their competitors. (Note that tips in these chains are substantially larger than at other restaurants with similar menus but without the emphasis on flirting—which may explain why even those who are not fond of flirting may seek to work in them.) For instance, restaurants that host bachelor parties are particularly likely to expect waitresses to flirt. If you choose to flirt, there is plenty of advice on offer, most of which we find problematic. If you work in a restaurant that wants you to flirt, but you opt not to, we suggest you learn to be a particularly engaging and chatty conversationalist. Have a stock of good jokes. Learn about the important sports teams in your area, and be ready to discuss them. Keep up on current events.

Men can certainly improve their tips by flirting, too, but the impact may be less than it is for women. Men's flirting skills are typically more in evidence, and presumably more valuable, in bartending roles.

Don't Overdo the Engagement

Although engaging with your guests is generally desirable, there are some circumstances in which you risk overdoing matters. When a restaurant is busy, long conversations with one table can annoy guests at other tables. Also bear in mind that you do not need to become friends with your guests. By all means be warm, friendly, and engaging, but do not feel the need to associate with them after your shift has ended.

Dealing With Fellow Employees

In general, the more helpful you are to fellow employees, the less trouble you'll have with them. Here are some further tips on dealing with your colleagues:

Wait Staff

In many team situations, one or more of the servers will be a weak link. They will under perform, either because they are new and untrained, less competent than the other team members, or simply lazy. You have a choice as to how to react to this. If the person is new, you can help train him. If he is just not very able, you will probably have to live with his lesser competence—or try to get him shifted to other responsibilities. The biggest problem is how to handle the lazy colleague. The worst thing you can do is to adopt his poor attitude. The best thing you can do is maintain your professionalism.

One way to get around the problem to some degree is to "buddy" with one other person on the floor. (See page 135 for more on this idea.) Another is to approach your manager for her help in improving the weak server's skills or attitude, or in finding a replacement.

Food Runners

Since food runners deliver to your tables the items your customers have ordered from you, their performance has an impact on your tips. Do not let your food runner approach your table with plates that he or she will try to auction—"Who has the salmon? The halibut? The swordfish?" Make sure your food runners know the seat assignments (north, south, etc.) and, for each table, which seat gets which dish.

BUSSERS

Do not annoy your busser. If you do, he may not take the trouble to clear and clean your tables quickly, meaning that you are unable to serve as many customers in a shift as you would like—or that you will have to do the dirty work yourself.

Don't treat your busser like your personal servant. Treat him like a partner—with respect. Your tips will depend upon how well your partnership functions. If he is a new busser, or not well trained, by all means train him. And be generous in compensating him. If you go the extra mile and introduce him to your tables, you may find he will be forever grateful.

If you know your busser would like to become a waiter, help him learn what is required.

HOSTS AND HOSTESSES

Hosts and hostesses are in charge of seating guests, which means they have considerable discretion as to which guests are seated in your section rather than someone else's, and in what order they seat guests in the various sections. A smart and considerate hostess can do you a favor by not seating two (or more) tables at exactly the same time in your section. A hostess who wants to help you can go further and seat high value guests in your section. High value here refers to guests who are likely to be easy to serve and who will presumably tip well. (The opposite: a party comprising messy, screaming infants or guests expected to tip badly.)

Consequently, being on very good terms with the hostesses can pay off mightily. Bear in mind, however, that many hostesses are low-paid high school students who have no restaurant experience and pay little attention to the details of what they are meant to do. As a result, even a hostess who likes you may fail to do a great job of helping you.

KITCHEN

Do not distract or annoy the chef by trying to talk with him when he's busy knocking out a series of dishes that require his complete concentration. If you do, he may not take the trouble to help you when you need a favor, such as cooking a dish in a peculiar fashion that your guest requires.

Since many servers only communicate with chefs when something is wrong—"the steak was too rare" or "the mashed potatoes were lumpy"—you can brighten a chef's day by giving a compliment when a customer really liked an item.

When dealing with the rest of the kitchen staff, always make your orders clear, whether they are written or spoken.

Treat the kitchen staff with respect. Thank them after a busy shift. Consider buying them a pitcher of beer occasionally as a thank-you.

BAR STAFF

You will want to stay on the right side of your establishment's bartender and cocktail waitresses so that you (and more importantly your customers) get the best service from them. Annoy your cocktail waitress and she may "forget" to bring your drinks or delay bringing them to your table, upsetting your customers who will likely blame you.

You may be able to score points by helping the bartender when he's busy by selecting the appropriate glasses, putting ice in those that require it, and adding the mixers or garnishes.

MANAGERS

If at all possible, cultivate your manager's goodwill. A manager who likes you and respects your work can help you in multiple ways, from giving a good station and shifts to rescuing you when you are in the weeds.

A manager recently promoted from waiter is likely to be a good first manager—aware of the difficulties of waiting tables, willing to provide training and advice, and not yet focused solely on the bottom line.

As is the case in any industry, it's never wise to go over the head of your manager (or lead server, or whomever else is meant to be your direct boss).

DATING FELLOW EMPLOYEES

Given that many servers spend a great deal of time with their fellow servers both on and off the job, it is hardly surprising that romantic (or purely sexual) relationships often spring up. Proximity makes it easy to find a partner, but it also means that the demise of a relationship can be particularly awkward. After a relationship fails, working next to an ex-lover can be extremely annoying. Colleagues are forced to take sides, which means that the work environment can become toxic. The server with the most seniority is likely to hang onto the best shifts and the relationships with other servers and managers, so the junior server may feel it would be good to change jobs. This is one of the reasons servers change jobs so frequently. Although it is relatively easy for an experienced server to change jobs, a history of jumping from one restaurant to another makes it very difficult to move up to the best restaurants, which invariably want reliable servers who are inclined to remain with their employers for long periods.

How Your Performance Will Be Judged

PERFORMANCE EVALUATION FORM

POOR	FAIR	AVERAGE	GOOD	EXCELLENT

Understanding Of Job: responsibilities, procedures, paperwork

☐	☐	☐	☐	☐

Comments: _____

Quality Of Service: fast, accurate, friendly

☐	☐	☐	☐	☐

Comments: _____

Productivity: time utilization, number of customers served

☐	☐	☐	☐	☐

Comments: _____

Upselling: encourages diners to add more (expensive) items to orders

☐	☐	☐	☐	☐

Comments: _____

Customers' Reactions: enjoy her service, often request her, tip well

☐	☐	☐	☐	☐

Comments: _____

Team Orientation: routinely helps others, alert to others' needs

☐	☐	☐	☐	☐

Comments: _____

Reliability: arrives on time, does not miss shifts, consistently does what job requires, not temperamental

☐   ☐   ☐   ☐   ☐

Comments: _____

Appearance: neat, well-groomed

☐   ☐   ☐   ☐   ☐

Comments: _____

Safety And Hygiene: obeys rules in food handling, personal hygiene

☐   ☐   ☐   ☐   ☐

Comments: _____

Attitude: toward customers, colleagues, supervisors, and job overall

☐   ☐   ☐   ☐   ☐

Comments: _____

Improvement Over Time: appreciates and seeks constructive criticism, pays attention to best practices of others

☐   ☐   ☐   ☐   ☐

Comments: _____

Overall Evaluation

☐   ☐   ☐   ☐   ☐

Comments: _____

GROUNDS FOR IMMEDIATE DISMISSAL

Some server behaviors are grounds for immediate dismissal. Keep in mind the dozen most common reasons restaurants fire waiters on the spot:

- Falsification of application details.
- Harming a guest, or threatening or attempting to do so.
- Being rude or unkind to a guest.
- Being intoxicated or under the influence of drugs during working hours.
- Missing a scheduled shift without management permission.

- Serving alcohol to someone clearly intoxicated or to a minor.
- Violating safety or hygiene procedures.
- Theft of restaurant equipment, property, or money.
- Requesting a tip from a guest without prior management approval.
- Adding a tip to a guest's bill without prior management approval.
- Deliberately not charging a guest for food or drink without management approval.
- Using or disclosing confidential restaurant information.

Ways To Improve Your Performance

Becoming a better waiter is more of a journey than a destination. You can continue to improve as long as you are in the profession. Start by analyzing what you do well and not so well at the moment (taking into account what your managers say about you), and focus on improving your weak spots.

Performance Reviews

Most people shy away from performance reviews because they are afraid to hear what they have been doing wrong or are simply unable to accept criticism. If you want to improve your performance, however, this is exactly what you should want, so ask for periodic performance reviews. You will benefit in several ways. Asking for a review shows that you want to improve and that you are very open to constructive criticism and advice. A manager who sees that you want to improve will almost surely value you for it and help you to do so. Requesting constructive feedback also shows that you are sufficiently confident in your performance that you want to take every opportunity to bolster your skills and knowledge. If you are working for a good manager, she will probably watch you with a critical and helpful eye, and give you suggestions as a coach would give an athlete.

Exercises to Enhance Your Performance

There are several "exercises" you can carry out to improve your performance. For example, you can play the role of the customer and critique the waiter or waitress serving you. Choose a restaurant similar to your own to visit for a meal and pay close attention to what your server does. See whether you can anticipate what she will do next—and think about whether you could do it better. If she asks, "Does anybody need another drink?" you'll note to yourself that you would have improved on that by asking, "Can I freshen anyone's drink?" Next, watch to see whether there are moments when your server misses an opportunity to sell you a drink or an upgrade. Ask yourself what you would have done to raise the bill or the potential tip. And pay close attention as well to what you and your friends want from your server. The more you think like a customer, the better able you'll be to satisfy your own guests.

Another exercise is to describe the food and wine anytime you are eating, whether in a restaurant or at home. You can do so in your head or, better yet, to a friend since having to speak out loud will improve your ability to pitch to customers in the future. Try to sell the food to her with your description. What are the ingredients? The method of preparation? What are the most interesting or impressive aspects of the dish? If you currently work or hope to work in an upscale restaurant, go beyond explaining the ingredients; explain why you like it. How does it make you feel? Adam claims that the beef dishes at Zazie make him feel warm, comforted, and nostalgic; the trout makes him feel fresh and light. At a high-end restaurant like Zazie, he often sells an "experience," not just a dish.

Learning From Others

Consider modeling your behavior—or at least altering your style a bit—by watching an expert server. Identify what she does particularly well, and then modify your own efforts based on her example.

Beyond that, consider what you can learn from someone who is willing to mentor you. A good mentor can show you how to do things differently, offer you constructive feedback on your efforts, and provide helpful suggestions as to how to plot your career. The most likely mentors are people senior to you in the restaurant and with whom you have a good relationship. The ideal mentor is good at her job, understands the restaurant (particularly the managers), and wants to help others progress.

Other Ways to Improve Performance

If you have fewer diners than usual on any given shift, take advantage of the opportunity to work on your skills, including your ability to more fully anticipate their desires, thereby giving them particularly fine service.

No matter what else you do to improve, you can almost surely learn more about your restaurant's food: what the ingredients are, where they come from, the methods of cooking employed, what distinguishes a dish from other similar dishes, and so on. In a similar manner, you can learn more about the drinks and wine your restaurant features.

You can also work on your technical skills, as discussed throughout this book. For example, try cross-training to learn what your colleagues are doing, whether they are in the front of the house (bussers, food runners) or back of the house (line and prep cooks).

Viewing Service from Your Guests' Perspective

Although you may think largely in terms of pleasing your manager, the satisfaction of your guests is the ultimate reflection of your performance as a server. Therefore, it can be helpful to view service from your guests' perspective. You can accomplish this by being a customer yourself and/or by interacting extensively with your guests during quiet periods. Ask them open-ended questions about what they do and don't like about the service in your restaurant and in others they have recently visited. Make it clear that you value what they are telling you by listening closely without multi-tasking, interrupting, or anticipating what they are going to say. Perhaps take some notes and ask additional questions to understand fully what they mean. Pay attention as well to what they don't say.

Imagine what a perfect experience would be for a guest at your restaurant, starting with the moment she walks through the door. Play out this scenario through being seated at the table, getting the menu, ordering, receiving each course, paying, and leaving. At which point is the service likely to be furthest from the guest's ideal? Where can you make a difference? Can you influence others, such as your busser, to improve service at other points in her dining experience?

CUSTOMER PET PEEVES

Customers are often tired, hungry, and therefore easily annoyed. Understanding what most often annoys them can help you please even the most demanding customers.

Lack of Attention/Laziness

- A *Food and Wine* survey of customers found that the top complaint was wait-staff disappearing during the meal. Nothing frustrates diners more than being unable to catch a waiter's attention when they would like to make a request or place an order.

- Food sitting in the pickup area and not being picked up.

- Server standing at the pick-up station waiting for an order to arrive instead of serving customers during the interval.

- Side dish is forgotten, either because waiter did not pick it up (and thus needs to go back to get it, after being reminded of it) or he failed to order it.

- Groups of waiters gathered together chatting rather than serving.

Unresponsiveness

- Being unresponsive to special needs. For instance, being dismissive of a Celiac sufferer's need to avoid any gluten.

Confusion

- Getting the wrong order.

- Servers not writing an order down and then having to check back to straighten it out.

- Not knowing what drink your customers are being served, especially when it comes to items they care greatly about. Imagine you are a diabetic and a waiter says, "I *think* this is the Pepsi and that one's the Diet Pepsi."

Lack of Knowledge

- Servers can't answer questions about the food or the restaurant.

- Servers can't recommend anything in particular— "Everything is good"—even when the food is not uniformly good.

Wasted Time

- Having to wait too long for the bill, or for change to be returned.

- Servers who waste their time telling customers about their personal lives, or bad-mouthing the restaurant or their boss and co-workers.

Cleanliness

- Sticky or wet table tops, condiment containers.

- Dirty waiter and busser uniforms or attire.

- Dirty or crumb-filled chairs.

- Menu is filthy—food or something else stuck on it.

Nuisances

- Being asked, "Do you need change?" when they have given an amount far in excess of the bill.

- Wobbly chairs and tables.

- Servers bothering them when they obviously want to be left in peace.

RESTAURANT PROFESSIONALS DISCUSS HOW YOU CAN IMPROVE

ADVICE FROM MANAGERS

"Maybe a guest wants pasta with a cream sauce. An average server will say, "It's not on the menu." A great server will say, "Let me talk with the chef and see what I can do for you."

Fine dining restaurant manager

"Pay attention: learn from the other servers with more experience."

Casual restaurant owner

"To move up, keep learning more about food and drink."

Casual restaurant chain manager

"Learn to multi-task. Learn to read your tables and anticipate what they will need next."

Casual restaurant chain manager-

"The key to making money differs. Some servers are very efficient; others are the big personality at the table; others are in-between."

Irish restaurant manager

"You need to learn the details and flourishes that you can provide to create the fine dining experience."

Steak house manager

"Excellent servers think several steps ahead. They prepare in advance, whereas average servers do one thing and then just stand around, thinking they've finished their work."

Asian restaurant manager

"You need to be able to interact with all sorts of customers."

Steak house manager

"People skills are essential; you need to be able to treat each guest differently."

Hotel restaurant manager

ADVICE FROM SERVERS

"Stay calm; whatever it is will be over in a few hours. Staying calm keeps the people around you calm."

Gastropub server

"Get in good with the kitchen, as they can fix your mistakes with little trouble."

Casual restaurant chain server

"A smile goes a long way."

Pub restaurant server

"The more organized you are, the easier the job is."

Pub restaurant server

"Take pride in everything you do."

Fine dining restaurant server

"Taste everything, all the way to the whiskey and cigars."

Fine dining restaurant server

"You need to approach the customers in a good mood or they won't feel good."

Pub restaurant server

"Keep moving—there is always something more that needs to be done."

Fine dining restaurant server

Legal Matters

Tips and Taxes

You are obligated to pay taxes on the amount you are paid by your restaurant and the amount you are tipped by guests—including tips paid in cash. To do so, you will need to keep a daily log of your tip income. Bear in mind that you do not need to pay taxes on the amount you give to other employees (such as a busser, food runner, hostess, or bartender) when you "tip out." Note that employers are permitted to deduct the cost of processing your credit card tip, but only the actual cost of processing it, which is likely to be 2—3 percent. They are not permitted to deduct any amount from your tips for their labor or overheads. But whatever amount is deducted from your earnings is not taxable to you.

Your employer will probably be required to file social security taxes on your earnings. If you do not notify your employer of your tip income, your employer obviously will not be able to report it. You may be held liable for this oversight and subject to a substantial penalty as a result.

Given employers' need to make social security payments on your behalf, you may be asked at the end of each shift how much you made in tips. Predictably, many waiters under-declare. At some restaurants, managers must sign off on a declaration of a certain percentage in tips. At a restaurant in a metropolitan area in which diners regularly tip 15—20 percent, the computers may be set to require managerial clearance for declaring less than 15 percent of total sales. In such a case, expect some waiters to declare tip income of a dollar or two over 15 percent, regardless of how much they actually received. Of course, as more tipping is done by credit card payment, waiters have less wiggle room as to what they declare as taxable income. We urge you not to take this approach. Waiters make easy IRS targets—and anyone who has ever been audited can attest to the awfulness of the experience.

(Please bear in mind that neither of the authors is a tax accountant or tax lawyer; the comments made here should not be considered legal, accounting, or tax advice.)

Should You Ever Sue Your Restaurant?

Waiters and other employees sue their restaurant employers for a number of reasons. Sometimes it's because they were hurt on the job and claim that their injuries would not have occurred if their employer had cleaned up the greasy floor or replaced the broken oven door. More often, though, waiters sue when they are not paid what they believe they are owed or when they are fired, arguably for inadequate cause. (Consult page 53, "How Servers are Paid," including the chart "Minimum Server Wages," for information about what servers are owed.)

You are certainly within your rights to sue if you believe you have been wronged. If you have not been paid what you are officially owed, in fact, we urge you to take whatever legal action is appropriate to collect your money.

However, it is worth bearing in mind that suing your employer may limit your ability to get other jobs in the industry. Employers sometimes check to determine whether you have sued your employer in the past. (Corporate restaurant groups and large restaurants are the most likely to do so.) While suing for back wages is unlikely to deter an honest employer from hiring you, a prospective employer who learns that you have sued for another reason will undoubtedly ask you to explain what happened. You may well persuade the employer that you were justified in suing, especially if yours was an egregious situation. On the other hand, some employers will shy away from hiring anyone who has previously sued an employer for non-wage reasons. This is particularly true for anyone who has sued multiple employers.

This book is not intended as a guide to your legal rights and obligations. If you believe you have been wronged, consult a lawyer as well as trusted family and friends, and then consider the potential trade-off between what you might win at trial or through the threat of a trial and the effect your suit might have on your future employability.

Changing Jobs

Chapter Seven

Getting Promoted

You may be content to be a waiter, and just want to focus on increasing your earnings (with the help of this book, of course). On the other hand, you may want to be promoted, whether to lead server, bartender, key holder, manager, or corporate manager.

You are likely to be considered eligible for a promotion if you:

- Are reliable.

- Hold your own as a server, requiring little if any support from management during your shifts.

- Make relatively few mistakes as a server.

- Are highly organized and efficient.

- Know the menu, the restaurant's operations, and the personnel.

- Have been at the restaurant for a considerable time. Seniority is a relative concept, of course, particularly in the restaurant world. At some restaurants the most senior server will have been there for only six months; at others, this half-year tenure would mark her out as the junior-most server.

- Have a positive and professional attitude.

Once you have identified the next step you are aiming for on the career ladder, evaluate what key skills, knowledge, and experience will be required to perform your target job. Compare that with your own skills, knowledge, and experience, and identify any gaps you need to fill. Armed with this information, develop a plan to acquire them. This can include:

- Watching and learning from those in the relevant positions.

- Adding responsibilities to your current job.

- Being mentored by one or more managers you respect.

- Helping those in your target position when you have free time.

- Possibly taking relevant courses (such as in bartending).

Learning the language of local kitchens, which is often Spanish, can also be an immense help. In large parts of the country general managers are expected to be fluent in Spanish to be able to communicate effectively with the whole staff.

SHOULD YOU BECOME A BARTENDER OR MANAGER?

BARTENDER

There are a number of reasons that people prefer to be bartenders instead of servers, including:

- As a rule of thumb, bartenders generally make 25—75% more than servers. The primary reason for this is that bartenders can be more efficient than servers. Bartenders need to move only a few feet to serve a guest, whereas servers need to go back and forth to the kitchen to do so. Bartenders also don't need to cater to children, who often order relatively little but require a great deal of time as well as patience.

- They have substantially more customer interaction. In addition to being enjoyable for extrovert bartenders, this also leads to larger tips.

- They enjoy greater status—with guests and with other employees.

The downsides to bartending are generally the later hours (bars often continue to serve even after the restaurant's kitchen has shut) and responsibilities, such as having to determine whether to continue to serve someone who is drunk, needing to break up fights, and so on.

MANAGER

Managers are generally paid an hourly (or sometimes a weekly) rate, possibly with bonuses added on based upon the volume of business done or other success factors. This can be attractive to those who want the security of knowing in advance what they will be paid, and not having their income vary from one week to the next. Managing other people, and seeing a complicated operation perform well, can also be very satisfying.

The downside to becoming a manager is that the security of having a set paycheck comes at a price: good servers often make more than their managers. The same is not true of poor servers—but they are seldom offered the chance to become managers.

Tips for getting a bartending job:

- Prove yourself as a server. Many restaurants hire bartenders from within, usually servers who are capable of interacting well with guests, serving efficiently with few mistakes, and not being overwhelmed by the typical stresses.

- Help the bartender before or after your shifts.

- Get experience as a college student by bartending at parties, in the faculty club, and so on.

- Take a bartending course.

If you decide that you would like to "move up" to a managerial position, you may make the leap directly from server to manager. In a large or corporate restaurant, however, you are more likely to move up in half-steps, starting perhaps as a lead server and then becoming a manager.

Be careful, however, if an owner or manager twists your arm to become a manager when you have shown no interest in the position. Although this may be because you are the only server with managerial capabilities, it may also be a red flag indicating that he or she is in over his head and desperately wants you to solve his problems. If you are approached about moving up but do not want to do so, communicate to management what you do want. For instance, you may want more or different shifts.

FINDING NEW CHALLENGES

You may not want to become a bartender or manager, but still need to stave off the feeling of monotony of doing the same thing each shift. One way to combat this is to focus on becoming the most professional and best server possible. Part of this effort will presumably involve learning more about the food and drink you serve. Another way to learn is to do something quite different periodically. Train other servers or work a few shifts in the kitchen on the line and in prep.

Appendix:
Brennan and Adam's Stories

Brennan's Step Up to Key Holder

Brennan decided to add to his serving duties at Eureka! in Berkeley California. He'd had experience at a series of Bay Area restaurants, including Papalote, Umami Burger, and Lanesplitters Pizza, before starting at Eureka! As he notes:

"I approached our general manager about key-holding, looking for experience more than anything. I wanted to get used to waiting for a paycheck and not relying on tips—they can be really good, but they can also be really inconsistent. I never thought about moving into management when I first started key-holding, but now that I'm starting to get more familiar with the management side of things, I'm actually trying to get into salaried management."

As for the biggest challenges of key-holding, he's found that "counting money, drawers, and doing the financial side of key-holding is super easy, but being the only 'management' type figure in the building when you have an angry guest is the scariest thing in the world. But you get used to it and just remember to be super polite."

He recognizes what merited him the promotion: "Being consistent is what landed me the key-holding gig. Knowing how to multi-task, to look at the whole restaurant as a chess board, and to look at everything going on while knowing how to speak with guests at the same time are the best qualities to help you get into key-holding."

Adam's Move Up to Manager

[Adam Murray, this book's co-author, moved up from server to manager after this book's first printing. Here are his reflections on how he did so.]

Through the process of researching and writing this book, I was made aware of the inner workings of restaurants from interviews with service workers and restaurant owners, as well as my own experiences serving, hosting, and bartending.

The most important change that resulted from this experience was the removal of my "server blinders," which kept me focused only on my tables and their individual needs, instead of looking at the function and flow of the restaurant as a whole.

Working on this book required mindfulness and analysis of my work space, which in turn made me aware of all aspects of the restaurant. As a result, I learned ways in which I could make my task list more efficient, while also helping my coworkers.

I learned that it is important to have at least a working knowledge of each position in the restaurant. This allows you to not only anticipate ways in which you can help out and make your coworkers job easier, but also promotes independence. Need your wine carafe washed but the dishwasher isn't around? Run it through the system yourself! Need a beer poured but the bartender is changing the keg? Pour it yourself! They will likely appreciate your ability to cover for them, as this is one less task they have to prioritize. I can't emphasize enough how much favor this has earned me over the years. This is something you can employ in your own work while you read this book. Look at the bigger picture at your restaurant. Where does service slow down or falter? Is there an opportunity to make you or your coworkers' workflow more efficient? If you make your colleagues' work lives easier, they are likely to return the favor.

While researching for this book, I was also gaining vital knowledge and skills that would ultimately help my career advance beyond waiting tables. In the time since the first printing of this book, I have been promoted to manager at Zazie. This position requires me to be able to do a little bit of everything, helping out at whichever station might need a push to keep up the speed of service. Sometimes this work isn't glamorous— glasses need to be washed, silverware polished and put away— but these tasks keep the momentum flowing and a good manager can spot where they should insert themselves to be most effective.

Another managerial benefit of working on this book was the relationships I fostered with my co-workers. Not surprisingly, through my time interviewing and working with the service staff, I grew closer to and developed stronger connections with my colleagues. This led to a smoother transition to the management position, as it is easier to lead a team that likes and respects you as a person. It can be easy to distance yourself from your team when you are a manager, since you may deal mostly in sales numbers and beverage order forms, but in my opinion, the connection you foster through face-to-face interactions with your staff can be your biggest asset as a manager. By being mindful of the whole restaurant, building relationships with coworkers, and showing up ready to make everyone's job smoother, you too could set yourself up for a promotion from server to management.

ADAM'S REFLECTIONS ON HIS FIRST MONTHS AS A MANAGER

Management

In my 3 months since being promoted to Manager, I have learned a good deal about the challenges of the new position. Unlike waiting tables, bussing, or running food, a manager's daily duties are much less straightforward, focusing on the big picture instead of the completion of routine tasks, such as taking orders, clearing plates, etc. As a manager, you need to examine your restaurant through many perspectives. A good manager should be able to, simultaneously, see the restaurant as a patron, as an employee, and as an owner, focusing on guest experience, team workflow, and big picture financials, respectively.

Guest Experience

One of the simplest yet most effective tools I have found while managing is to sit down at an empty table during service. It is amazing how your perspective changes when you are looking at the restaurant from that of a guest. When I am sitting, I am better able to notice music levels, discrepancies in lighting, and recognize when employees are being too loud and raucous for the environment. This switch-up of perspective is a tool I am working on honing further, hoping to ultimately be able to notice these differences while still actively engaged with the workflow of the restaurant.

It is also important to touch base with the guests themselves, asking them about the food, the service, and their experience overall. I have found that by opening this line of communication directly with the guests, you can earn their trust and learn aspects of their dining experience that you wouldn't hear about otherwise. This strategy is especially effective with regulars, as they know what to expect and can explain specific differences from one night to another.

Team Workflow

A more difficult aspect of switching from service to management was to change the way I view downtime at the restaurant. Even the busiest of establishments have moments during service in which the servers are all "caught up" and don't have any immediate tasks they need to get done. When I was a server, I would see these times as moments to chat, catch up, or grab a bite to eat. As a manager, it is my goal to continue to make the servers feel as if these moments are "breaks" while also pushing them to get some side work done that will benefit the restaurant as a whole. For example, last night was particularly slow at Zazie. The servers were chatting, having attended to their tables, so I brought napkins to them to fold, and I worked with them while they talked. By engaging in the work with them, and showing them that they can still have a good time while getting some extra work done, I was able to turn down time into catch-up time, and decrease work that the same staff would have to do later on a busier evening.

Another aspect of team workflow I have focused on is conflict resolution. Restaurants can oftentimes be a breeding ground for resentment between employees, whether spurred by servers upset about smaller sections, or miscommunications with the kitchen staff. It is my job to get everyone on the same page, help them feel appreciated for their work, and ultimately resolve ongoing conflicts in the interest of maintaining a healthy work environment for everyone involved. At a place like Zazie, which values employee retention, it is of the utmost importance that I catch these moments before they bubble up into a conflict that can't be easily resolved. Helping staff open communication with basic "I feel" statements has gone a long way to ensuring we don't have employees fed up with their coworkers to the point of quitting.

Big Picture

Perhaps the hardest change in perspective for me to wrap my head around is seeing the restaurant as if I were the owner, focusing on food cost, labor, comps, and waste. As a server, it was often in my best interest to get items comped off the bill, as it would usually result in a better tip for me. Now, as manager, it is my job to approve these comps, and make sure that everything we give away is in the best interest of the company as a whole. For example, if a server makes a mistake and wants to buy a round of drinks for the table, I will first have the server formally apologize for the mistake and see if recognition of the mistake is enough for the table to feel validated. While everyone loves "free" things, guiding servers to own up to their mistakes instead of bandaging them with free drinks is better for the restaurant in terms of food cost and the employees' understanding of what is expected of them. If they work through the uncomfortable moment of verbally apologizing, they are less likely to repeat the mistake than if I allowed them to fix everything with free food and drink. As a manager, it can be hard for me to push my employees towards this kind of resolution, but it holds them accountable and is in the best interest of the business.

The most satisfying aspect of looking at the company in this way is the information I am able to share with the owners to help the restaurant grow and thrive. In my meeting with the owners I have the unique role of representing the desires and concerns of my employees, having recently been in their position myself. I push myself to think like an employee in these meetings, just as I try to think like an owner during nightly service. Having a foot on each side gives me a valuable perspective— a more complete view of the restaurant than was accessible to me when I was just a waiter.

I am still learning more about ways to improve in my role as manager, but so far these tools have been a great help as I push forward in this career.

CHANGING RESTAURANTS

If you are not earning a great deal (in spite of following this book's advice) and your restaurant does not treat you very well, you may benefit from considering a change of employers. Before rushing to quit your current job, however, slow down and gather some useful information.

Do a careful analysis of how much you make per hour and in total. Factor your transportation and waiting time, if any, in your per-hour calculation. Analyze, too, what you like and dislike about the job. Then organize your information about this job and likely alternatives. Here are some questions to ask yourself about your current job:

- How much do you enjoy going to work each day?

- How much pride do you take in your work and in your restaurant?

- How are you treated by your managers and fellow employees?

- How much effort is required of you—on the job, and getting to and from the job?

- How much money do you make (and how much free food and drink do you consume)?

- How flexible are management and your colleagues in meeting your needs? For example, do you get the number and nature of shifts you want?

Then consider what other jobs you might like to land:

- What other restaurants might you want to work at?

- How much do you know about them? About working there?

- How do they rate in terms of work conditions, location (including your commute), pay, and any other factors important to you?

Compare your current job with the other jobs you might be able to get. If your current job does not compare favorably, take appropriate steps to find out more about the other jobs. (See the discussion in Chapter 1 especially in "Types of Restaurant," for more about assessing a job.)

Leaving a Job

Giving Notice

You are generally expected to give two weeks' notice before leaving your employment. Many waiters make the mistake of quitting on the spot and failing to put in their two weeks. This has several unfortunate consequences. It eliminates your chances of returning to work there if something does not work out at your new job. It also greatly reduces your chances of getting a positive reference from the restaurant. On a less obvious level, it makes it awkward to return to the restaurant to drink or dine. On the other hand, if you do serve out your two weeks (and continue to perform at your usual quality level), you are likely to be treated very well if you return to dine there. When one of our friends returns to dine at a former restaurant of his, he is never charged for everything he orders—his entire meal is comped by his former manager.

Exit Interviews

You may have an exit interview when you depart your restaurant. From your employer's perspective, this will be designed to understand why you are leaving. This gives your employer an opportunity to learn from you departure and possibly to consider changing how it operates. Departing employees tend to be more forthcoming about what the restaurant does poorly than current employees may be. Not all restaurants take advantage of the opportunity, of course, whether because they already know why you are leaving (your chance to star in a TV series or, more mundanely, because you are moving) or because they do not want to hear any criticism, no matter how well founded.

From your perspective, a departure interview is an opportunity to offer constructive feedback and thereby help your employer. Many departing employees, however, make the mistake of seeking revenge for real or supposed poor treatment by their managers and others.

Resist this temptation. You are likely to encounter your manager and other colleagues in the future, so there is no sense in antagonizing anyone.

If you sense your interviewer is being forced to interview and is not interested in learning anything from you, simply offer the usual platitudes about why you are leaving rather than offering even highly constructive criticism. You might say you have a better opportunity elsewhere, can no longer commit to the necessary hours, need to focus on your school work, etc. On the other hand, if your interviewer really does want constructive criticism, offer helpful comments in a calm and objective manner.

Departure Forms

Corporate restaurants—and those that have been sued by waiters in the past—are likely to ask you to sign a form acknowledging that you are not leaving:

- Because of anything the restaurant, managers, or fellow employees did

- Pursuant to medical advice

- To escape unsafe working conditions.

This helps the restaurant prevent future lawsuits. If you do not have a reason to sue, and are not intending to do so, feel free to sign the document. On the other hand, if there is a possibility that you might wish to sue the restaurant or one of its managers or other employees in the future, do not sign it as it will count heavily against your chances of winning a lawsuit.

MAKING A GRADUAL SHIFT TO ANOTHER RESTAURANT

You may want to continue working at one restaurant even after you've been hired at another. There are good reasons to take this cautious approach. At some restaurants, you will not be considered a permanent employee until you have worked there for some period of time, often 90 days. As a result, you may not want to quit your current job in case the new restaurant does not work out. To manage the transition, you will need to drastically limit your shifts at your current restaurant. And you may need to limit your shifts at your new restaurant, too, but this will be tricky because you will want to show your new employer that you are a flexible and eager employee. In some instances, of course, this won't be a real issue because your new restaurant may not have a lot of shifts for you immediately.

YOU AREN'T A CAREER WAITER, ARE YOU?

If you are relatively young and work in an upscale restaurant, you are likely to receive job offers from some of your customers. For whatever reason, many customers will assume you are waiting tables while hoping to realize your actual ambitions. Consequently, they will suggest that you consider working for them in some customer service or other position. And of course film and TV producers have long offered jobs to dazzling-looking servers, although this is a lot more likely in New York or Los Angeles than it is in Kokomo or Kalamazoo. Fielding offers from your customers may or may not be a job perk, depending on how much you like waiting tables—and the quality of the jobs you're offered.

GETTING A JOB IN AN UPSCALE RESTAURANT

Many upscale restaurants hire largely on the basis of attitude and personality, but some also require substantial experience.

If you have targeted a restaurant for which your current experience is insufficient, or your background is not sufficiently compelling in some other regard, there are six steps you can take to improve your odds of employment substantially.

Get the most relevant job possible. You have several options. You could work as a waiter in a fine dining or high-volume upscale (or even casual) restaurant anywhere, or in a college faculty club. If that is not possible, work as a waiter in a neighborhood restaurant or equivalent. Or work as a hostess, busser, food runner, or bar back in your target restaurant. Better yet, do so in a restaurant in that group. For instance, in New England, one organization owns Smoke House, Hemenway's, and numerous other local restaurants. Performing well at the Smoke House will help you move up to one of the group's fancier restaurants, such as The Mooring, where the average bill is approximately triple that at the Smoke House, or Castle Hill Inn, one of the country's fanciest hotels.

If you work in a non-serving capacity (such as a busser) in your target restaurant, bear in mind that it will probably not help you get desirable serving jobs in other restaurants. Thus, you need to consider how important and likely it is that your target restaurant would hire you as a server after you've worked there as a busser. Evaluate the following factors to determine whether working in a non-serving capacity would make sense:

- Whether your target restaurant prefers to hire servers internally (from its ranks of bussers, etc.) rather than selecting those with serving experience elsewhere.

- How frequently serving positions become available at this restaurant. (Note that in some highly desirable restaurants servers stay for dozens of years because they value their positions so highly.)

- How many other bussers, hosts, and the like you will be competing with for the next available server position, and how readily you will be able to out-perform them and thereby get to the head of the queue.

- Your pay as a busser, host, food runner or bar back versus what you could earn as a server elsewhere.

- How much you expect to eventually make working as a server in your target restaurant versus what you could make in other restaurants.

Develop the skills critical to your target job. The skills discussed throughout this book, especially in Chapters 4 and 6, are those most essential to performing well at an upscale restaurant. Try to eat at your target restaurants to learn which skills will be most important, then evaluate your own skills in light of what you have learned and work on those that need to be improved.

In addition, make sure your attitude is also consistent with working at an outstanding restaurant. Note how many restaurants hire more on the basis of personality—sociability, positive attitude, warmth, and ability to converse with guests—than skill.

OTHER VALUABLE SKILLS

Speaking a relevant second language with proficiency makes you more valuable for restaurants of that variety (Italian, French, etc.) and makes you more appealing to guests who speak that language.

Cross-training so that you can perform multiple functions means a restaurant has less to worry about when someone does not show up for his shift.

Having life-saving skills can also be of value. You can be Red Cross-certified in first aid and CPR (cardiopulmonary resuscitation). Better yet, though, would be EMT (emergency medical technician) training and certification.

Make your skills and attitude apparent to your managers in order to get the best recommendations. Develop a strong relationship with one or more managers, whether current or past supervisors of your work, in order to get strong recommendations. Consider what your managers would consider most valuable. Think about what your managers most often find exasperating in their servers, you in particular. If nothing else, demonstrate a strong team orientation.

Learn which restaurants to target. You may already know which are the premier restaurants in your area, but you will want to go beyond this to understand what working at each of them would involve, and which would be the best fit for your personality and work style. See page 48 for more about how to discover the necessary information.

Come to the notice of these excellent restaurants. If you have been diligent in your networking efforts (see page 63 for more about networking), you may already have contacts at your target restaurants—people who can both attest to your abilities and introduce you to those in charge of hiring. If not, get busy networking. Another possibility is to work at a restaurant or bar that is a late night gathering place for people in the restaurant trade. Be especially professional and friendly with them. If you serve these people well, when a slot opens at their restaurants, they will be inclined to recommend you for the job. Their recommendation is worth a great deal. Even corporate restaurants value knowledgeable recommendations more than almost any other sort of information.

Develop your ability to market yourself well. Work on your interviewing skills, practice your elevator pitch, polish your resume, and put together a persuasive cover letter. Learn as much as possible about your target restaurant, including its history, menu, and clientele. (Consult Chapter 1, "Types of Restaurant," for more regarding what you should know about a restaurant.)

EDUCATION AND REFINEMENT

If you want to work in an elegant establishment, it will help if you look and sound highly educated and refined. For example, a senior manager of a national steak house chain told us, "At Applebee's, it's 'guys' serving 'guys.' Here, it's ladies and gentlemen serving ladies and gentlemen." In other words, the ideal server is someone who appears to be upper-middle class. To appear more upper-class and elegant, consider consulting the extensive etiquette literature, particularly the sections on dress, speech, manners (especially table manners), and hosting. The following are all valuable resources:

- Colleen Rush, *The Mere Mortal's Guide to Fine Dining: From Salad Forks to Sommeliers: How to Eat and Drink in Style without Fear of Faux Pas.* An extremely useful introduction to fine dining. Highly recommended

- Dorothea Johnson and Liv Tyler, *Modern Manners: Tools to Take You to the Top.* An excellent general guide to manners. Recommended

- Kelly Williams Brown: *Gracious: A Practical Primer on Charm, Tact, and Unsinkable Strength.* An old-fashioned and charming treatment of how to be gracious. Recommended

- Two short books aimed at a younger audience's need to learn proper table manners and the like are also recommended: Walter Hoving (the former director of the Metropolitan Museum) wrote *Tiffany's Table Manners for Teenagers* years ago, but it is still a fine primer. So, too, is Dorothea Johnson's *The Little Book of Etiquette.*

- If you want to become truly expert on cutlery, plates and other dishes, consult *The Art of the Table,* by Suzanne von Dranchenfels, which provides a detailed guide to selecting, laying, using, and maintaining elegant tableware.

Although no one book is an ideal guide to style, the following are useful primers:

- Andrea Pomerantz, *How to Look Expensive: A Beauty Editor's Secrets to Getting Gorgeous without Breaking the Bank.* A style guide for women.

- G. Bruce Boyer, *True Style: The History and Principles of Classic Menswear.*

- The 1980s best-sellers by John T. Molloy, *Dress for Success* (a style guide for men) and *Woman's Dress for Success,* are inevitably dated, but still useful in describing what constitutes upper-middle class attire.

If you are blessed with some well-mannered and charming friends, by all means pay attention to how they dress and act. And if you are a fan of old Hollywood movies, watch Cary Grant and other classy stars in action.

The easiest ways to increase your "refinement quotient" in an interview are to:

- Dress in an upper-middle class fashion.

- Take care of your grooming. Upscale restaurants tend to notice even the minutest grooming failures: nails not entirely clean and properly trimmed; stains of any sort on hands or clothing; shoes not polished; and so on.

Speak the part, too:

- Eliminate *like* and *you know* (or *ya know*) from your speech

- Pronounce the "g" at the end of words. Thus, eating rather than eatin', doing rather than doin', and so on. Banish the even more casual forms of common words, too, especially gonna, wanna, and cuz. Prefer going to, want to, and because.
- Use please, thank you, and you're welcome freely.
- Address your interviewer as sir or ma'am.

WHEN WORKING, YOU CAN ADD AN ELEGANT TOUCH IN OTHER WAYS:

- Do not interrupt conversations if you can avoid doing so. Wait for a pause, or until one or more guests turn to you to hear what you have to say.
- Instead of indicating where something is with a thrust of your head, or a curt, "It's over there," try "Let me show you."
- When asked for something, rather than saying "no problem" (you're doing your job, so a simple request should not be a problem) or "okay," say, "it's my pleasure" or "a pleasure." If you are working in a casual environment where those expressions would sound too formal, responding with "you bet" would be a good, informal alternative.
- Instead of "That's someone else's job," say, "Let me get the person who's most knowledgeable about that.
- Instead of asking, "Are you still working on that?" which suggests that dining is a chore rather than a pleasure, ask simply, "Are you still enjoying your meal, or shall I remove that plate?"
- Refer to men as gentlemen and women as ladies. Do not refer to a man as a guy or a dude, nor a woman as a girl or chick.

Making More Money

Chapter Eight

Selling More Food and Up-Selling

Given that most customers base their tips on how much they spend, increasing their spending will increase your tips. In general, there are two ways to get them to spend more: by having them buy more items, or having them buy more expensive items, a practice known as "upselling."

Selling More Food

There are innumerable ways to get diners to order more items than they had initially intended to purchase. You should approach guests with a desire to sell—but not with a high-pressure approach. Instead, you will be guiding them to products that they will greatly enjoy.

It's helpful to assume your guest wants a drink, a full meal, including an appetizer, dessert, and so on. Rather than asking, "Did you want an appetizer?" ask, "Which of our appetizers has caught your eye?" Or, "Which one of our appetizers is irresistible tonight?" Or, "Can I help you choose an appetizer?"

Encourage a guest to order a more complete meal. Thus, if a guest orders just a hamburger, ask whether he would like fries, a salad, or a vegetable, too. Or if she orders the fish entrée, ask whether she would care to have an appetizer. This is particularly effective if what the guest orders will take time to prepare. After telling her that her entrée will take 25 minutes to cook, ask if she would like to have some soup or an appetizer beforehand.

Appetizers

Suggest a specific appetizer or two that compliments the entrée. For instance, if a dedicated Italian foodie has ordered a veal entrée, mention the minestrone soup that is a house specialty. For someone who has ordered the Dover sole, an expensive, elegant and refined choice, mention something comparable as an appetizer, such as the lobster bisque.

Adding To Main Dishes

Know what additions you can offer to standard orders. If your restaurant serves serious steaks and charges extra for sauces, ask the guest ordering the porterhouse steak which sauce she would like—the béarnaise, port reduction, truffle butter, or peppercorn sauce. Then ask whether she would like the onion strings, thick-cut fries, or mashed potatoes. The grilled vegetables, asparagus, or creamed spinach. Perhaps a side salad—tomato and onion or simple green. And of course the easiest accompaniment to sell to a steak-eater is a glass—or even a bottle—of red wine.

In fact, many food items are improved with add-ons. A salad could have chicken, steak, or tuna added to it, just as a hamburger could have bacon for an additional price. Give guests a chance to add such items.

Desserts

Instead of asking in a general way whether guests would like to order dessert, mention the desserts available, preferably with a brief and appetizing description of them, and note which are the restaurant's top sellers if it's appropriate. When you ask, "Will there be anything else?" a guest is unlikely to order dessert. If you instead ask, "What would you like for dessert? We have some gorgeous chocolate cake, made with Belgian chocolate—and many of our guests like to add some French vanilla ice cream to it" you are much more likely to get an order.

Many guests will resist ordering any dessert because of their desire to avoid the calories. If your guests seem reluctant, ask if they would like to order a dessert "for the table" that they can all share. Similarly, you can note that each dessert does come with multiple forks and they are welcome to split an order. And if that doesn't work, consider asking whether they'd like to get a dessert to take home with them—just to make sure they don't get ravenous later on and face the inevitable craving for one of your incredible desserts.

Another approach to selling a dessert may be less obvious than pushing the double chocolate cake. If your guests have not yet finished a bottle of wine they ordered for their main course, you can help them enjoy the remainder of it by recommending a cheese that would match well with it.

Food Descriptions

Have luscious descriptive phrases for every menu item. If you use terms such as savory, tasty, smooth, spicy, or creamy, you may indirectly persuade diners to purchase items.

- Homemade
- Fresh daily
- Entirely from scratch
- Will serve two comfortably
- Made for sharing
- Suitably aged
- Natural
- Organic
- Locally-sourced
- Tangy
- Crunchy
- Crisp
- Tender
- Savory
- Extra large
- Jumbo
- Heaping
- Overflowing
- Award-winning
- Legendary
- The chef's grand-mother's recipe
- A variation on the traditional
- Extraordinary
- Traditional recipe
- Old-fashioned
- Original recipe
- Unique
- Incredibly popular
- Guests' favorite
- My favorite
- Char-broiled
- Lightly-breaded
- Melted cheese
- Well-spiced
- Marinated
- Piping hot

Be able to describe dishes in detail. "Our paella is almost as good as having it on a beach in Valencia. It has over half a pound of fresh shrimp, scallops, and squid, along with chorizo. The short-grained calasparra rice is imported from Spain. It's cooked in a special paella pan that allows the chef to create a great socarrat—the crust at the bottom that you get when you order this in Valencia, but nowhere else in this area."

SELLING OUT OF SEQUENCE

Don't give up too easily. You can often sell items out of the "natural" sequence. Even if a table did not order appetizers initially, you can still ask them again before the entrées arrive. "Your order is in and the food should be ready in fifteen minutes. Would you like some soup or a salad beforehand?" Similarly, a table may not have ordered wine when they ordered their meal, but you can certainly ask when you bring the appetizers whether they'd like to look at the wine list.

When you deliver the food, ask whether your guests would like something else at this time. Suggest additional drinks or a bottle of wine.

Given that unoccupied time passes more slowly than occupied time, you have every reason to help guests fill their time with food. To those guests who are waiting for their entrées, suggest some appetizers that can be brought immediately.

SPECIAL OCCASIONS

Whenever you see people celebrating something, suggest a bottle of champagne (or a half-bottle). It's also easier to get them to order dessert because the usual rules of frugality and weight-watching are likely to be suspended. "Given that it's a birthday celebration, I'm sure you've saved room for some chocolate cake." "I know a great way to top off a celebration like this—our fabulous lemon cheesecake—or our apple pie a la mode."

MAKING RECOMMENDATIONS

Diners will often ask what you recommend. Typical questions include:

- What is the best thing on the menu?
- What's good tonight?
- What is your favorite item?
- What would you recommend that isn't too fattening? Or that is gluten-free?

The rest of this book has concrete suggestions regarding how to suggest appropriate appetizers, wine, and so on. Beyond that, however, there are a few points to keep in mind:

- Find out as much as you can about your guests' preferences, because it is much easier to recommend food, for example, when you know that a guest loves spicy rather than bland food.
- Suggesting just a few items makes it easier for guests to choose—and, if done well, they'll choose more quickly and with gratitude for having their decisions made easier.
- If you are pressed for your personal favorites, feel free to give them—but if your tastes are not mainstream, add a caution that these are your very personal preferences (perhaps noting what in particular you like about a dish), and then go on to name customer favorites.
- Try to avoid saying that "everything here is good." This response does not give guests the help they want in making decisions.

Do not:
- Bad-mouth a food item your customer orders—"Ugh, I can't stand red meat. How can you eat an animal?"
- Tell a guest you don't like the taste of a particular dish. Instead, mention one you prefer, or note what most customers prefer.
- Get upset if a diner does not take your suggestion.

The Importance of Priming and Framing

Various experiments have demonstrated that how you phrase something has an impact upon how people think. This "priming" of people has a place in your serving repertoire. For instance, if you mention early on that a guest should save room for the spectacular chocolate desserts, you are priming her to say yes to dessert later. Similarly, the likelihood of a guest ordering wine is substantially increased by a waiter suggesting wine.

One savvy manager regards "drink," "appetizer," and "dessert" as swear words. She insists that her servers use specifics to paint an attractive picture instead of relying on these generic terms. Thus, they ask "Would you like a Long Island Iced Tea or Blue Hawaiian" instead of "Would you like a drink."

Your behavior and language can also affect the mood of your guests. If you are smiling, upbeat, and dynamic, your behavior will tend to shift your guests to your mood. Similarly, if you discuss happy events that have just occurred ("Can you believe the Tigers won today? Isn't that great?") or are about to occur ("The forecast for the weekend is dry and sunny!"), you are likely to improve the mood of the table. If they're upbeat, they'll be easier to serve. They will also leave better tips. And, by the way, the more that you play the part of an upbeat, positive person, the more you will feel that way yourself.

Up-Selling

Good up-selling involves understanding what guests like and what they are in the mood for—and then guiding them to choose the food or drink that is most likely to please them. From their perspective, they will have gotten excellent service.

In general, this will be easiest with a regular customer. The more you know about his likes and dislikes, the more you will be able to please him with suggested food and drink items. For instance, if you know that he likes to eat oily fish because of the health benefits, you can tell him that the restaurant has just gotten some gorgeous fresh mackerel that the chef would be happy to prepare in various ways which you would be happy to describe.

Even when you're not at all familiar with the tastes of a first-time guest, you can make some reasonably accurate estimates of his or her preferences as you gain experience in "reading a table." (See page 141 for more on this.)

When suggesting food or drink, offer two or three choices. More than three and guests are likely to be a bit overwhelmed and therefore indecisive, but offering just one feels like you are mandating what they should order. Note that helping guests make up their minds quickly has the added benefit of turning tables more rapidly, too.

There is an art to up-selling. The key is to be—and seem—helpful rather than pushy. For example, if a guest orders a vodka martini, you can ask, "Would you prefer Absolut, Grey Goose, or the house vodka?" This will provide subtle encouragement for her to order a specific brand (at a higher price than that of the house vodka), but also make it simple for her to opt for the house vodka. In other words, you are encouraging rather than arm-twisting.

Ideal Situations For Up-Selling

It is highly appropriate to suggest something higher priced when a diner is uncertain of what to order. If he mentions that he feels in the mood for some meat and then asks, "How are the burgers?" feel free to praise them, but then add that the sirloin steaks are a meat-lovers' dream.

It is similarly easy to pitch a higher-priced item as if you can solve a guest's dilemma of being unable to choose between different items. For example, if a guest is undecided between meat and fish, you can suggest the "surf and turf," which includes one of each at a higher price than either alone.

If you are dealing with tourists, keep in mind what the region or locale specializes in. If yours is a New England seafood restaurant, perhaps you should be discussing the lobster or steamed clams. In South Carolina, the shrimp and grits are the prized local fare. And so on.

Specials

Specials are generally more expensive than many of the other dishes on the menu. Labeling them as special gives servers a way to sell the dish. Diners have been conditioned to expect specials and will often ask for them. As a result, specials are often an easy sell. If there are no specials at a restaurant, consider mentioning the general specialty of the restaurant. For instance, at a Baltimore restaurant serving tourists, you could mention that the restaurant specializes in local crab. People like to feel they are ordering something special, so whatever you do to satisfy this urge is likely to be successful.

Many restaurants offer specials because they have more of a particular item than they need. For instance, a restaurant may have purchased a large amount of beef in anticipation of a large group of meat-hungry visitors coming to the restaurant. If it turned out that the group was in fact largely vegetarian, the restaurant may feature beef specials for the next few days. In some cases, it will offer servers free meals or cash bonuses to whoever sells the most of these specials. In any event, selling a lot of specials should please your manager.

UP-SERVING

In addition to up-selling, try up-serving. In other words, take whatever extra steps are necessary to give guests a great experience. This may mean encouraging them to contact you if they don't like every dish and glass you serve them—or if the service is less than perfect. Or checking to make sure that you know what changes they would prefer if they were to direct the chef on how to prepare the same dishes next time they visit. Up-serving not only gives you valuable feedback as a server, but can also increase your base of loyal and regular customers.

GENERAL STRATEGY

So when should you try to sell extra courses (appetizer, dessert) to tables, when should you aim to sell the most expensive items to your tables, and when should you try to turn tables as quickly as possible? The rules are simple:

When your restaurant or your station is busy, maximize the sale of expensive entrées and wine while still aiming to turn tables in rapid order. If the kitchen is overwhelmed but the bar is not, maximize the sale of drinks. When the restaurant is not busy, maximize the sale of all items, particularly including appetizers, desserts, and after-dinner drinks.

TRACKING
YOUR PERFORMANCE

If you track which guests order these items, you will be able to sell the same thing or something pricier to them the next time they come in. "As I recall, ma'am, the last time you were here you started with a Tanqueray gin and tonic. May I get you the same thing tonight?"

To improve your overall service, and especially your up-selling, keep track of what you sell each shift. If your restaurant's POS system does not collect the relevant data, put together a simple tracking sheet or copy this one:

DATE	MON	TUES	WED	THUR	FRI	SAT	SUN
Shift (lunch, dinner)							
Number of diners							
House drinks before meal							
Call drinks before meal							
Appetizers							
Specials							
Entrees							
Side dishes							
Glasses of wine							
Tables ordering 2nd bottle/wine							
Desserts							
Dessert specials							
After-dinner drinks							
Coffee, tea							

When you get back to your station, simply mark down the number of each item you have sold. Consolidate this at the end of the shift by showing the totals and perhaps entering them into your electronic device when you get home. Over time you should get a very clear picture of what you sell most effectively. You can then work on improving your technique to sell the other items more effectively.

Tracking what you sell will also develop your understanding of what you can and cannot sell effectively on particular shifts. For instance, you may find that you can sell bottles of wine by the dozen on Friday nights, but not on Wednesdays, when you might be better off suggesting half bottles.

[Note the implications of the above regarding "running your own business." See Chapter 9, p. 241.]

IMPACT UPON YOUR EARNINGS

How much impact can all of this have on your own income? Assume you wait on 30 people per shift. If you sell:

- 2 "call" drinks (rather than house or well drinks) to 4 guests = $40
- 6 extra drinks while guests wait for their food to arrive = $45
- 2 extra bottles of (relatively inexpensive) wine = $46
- 5 extra desserts = $45
- 3 extra after-dinner drinks = $36
- 6 extra appetizers = $54
- 6 extra side dishes (vegetables) = $30
- 6 specials (or higher priced entrées), priced at $4 more than what otherwise would have been ordered = $24

The total you have added to your guests' bills is $320. Assuming you get 20% as a tip, you just added some $64 to your earnings. If you work 5 shifts per week, you will have earned an extra $320 each week. Admittedly, this example is unrealistic if you work the breakfast shift in a diner. But if you work in a reasonably up-market restaurant it is exceedingly realistic. In fact, if you serve more guests, work in a pricey restaurant, or are simply better at up-selling, you could earn considerably more.

Turning Tables

One of the key factors in how much money you will make as a server is how quickly you can turn tables. In a busy restaurant, the more times tables can be turned, the greater the revenues and profits will be. Even in a less busy restaurant, you may be able to handle more guests than other servers do if your tables are ready for them. The following suggestions should help.

Start your shift by having everything in readiness. Complete all your side-work. Be aware of the likely demand you'll face that shift. If it's Friday night and your restaurant is emphasizing fish specials, you'll want to have extra lemons sliced. If the local college has an alumni gathering, perhaps you'll serve many more guests than usual, necessitating extras of everything be prepared.

Customers often don't know what they want. You have an opportunity to make life easier for them by suggesting two or three likely choices. Research indicates that guests follow such suggestions approximately 70 percent of the time, so you can speed them through the ordering process.

Bear in mind that selling a bottle of wine to a table is much more efficient than selling individual glasses. You minimize the number of trips to the table, plus you don't have to wait on your bartender to pour each glass. The same, of course, goes for a pitcher of beer rather than individual servings.

If you ring in food at the appropriate times, you can avoid having guests stuck at their tables waiting for lengthy periods without food. The usual time to submit an entrée order is immediately after appetizers arrive at the table. If you fail to do so, you are likely to delay the serving of the entrées and thus the completion of the meal.

Minimize your trips to the table by anticipating diners' needs. If someone orders white wine or champagne, find the ice bucket and then get the wine. Clear room on the table before you bring out the food. Bring the bibs and tiny shellfish forks when you bring the lobster to the table.

When you enter the dining room, scan your station to see who needs something. This will allow you to maximize each trip to your tables. For example, grab some extra lemon wedges for the table which is halfway through their fish entrées and signaling that they need more lemons so you don't need to make an extra trip for something so small and easily carried. If you develop the habit of scanning your station every time you enter the dining room, you'll know in what order to approach each of your tables, starting with those who have a problem with their order. You'll also short-circuit the major complaint diners have—that they cannot find their waiter when they need him during the meal.

Note, too, that the more regulars you serve, the fewer trips you'll need to make. You will know that Lisa likes balsamic vinaigrette on the side, Vivek and Atul want pepper cracked over their steaks but have no interest in parmesan cheese added to their pasta, Ming wants appetizer and entrée brought at the same time, and so on. As a result, you can anticipate their needs and minimize the number of trips you need to make to their tables.

If your busser is overwhelmed, you can accelerate the turning of tables by pre-bussing—periodically removing plates, glasses, and cutlery that your customers have finished using.

When a customer has finished her meal and is ready to pay, immediately give her the bill and complete the payment process. This will not only make the table available, it will also please your customer, given that she has better things to do than to wait for you to drop off a check and process her payment.

If you wish to encourage a table to leave, do so subtly. Ask, "Will there be anything else this evening?" If there is not, simply mention "I'll just leave the check here so it's ready when you are." Or you can simply leave the check on the table, without interrupting the table's conversation to do so.

TURNING TABLES IS NOT ALWAYS POSSIBLE

At some restaurants it will prove nearly impossible to turn tables rapidly. At a Maryland-style crab house, for instance, a typical diner may take two to three hours to consume a crab dinner. (One of the authors recently tried his best to consume a minimum blue crab order at Joe's Crab Shack in less than two hours and failed. This did not include the time required to study the menu, order the food, learn how best to open up the crab, and pay for the meal. The total dining experience took well over two-and-a-half hours.)

Getting The Best Shifts And Station

Identifying the Best Shifts

At nearly all restaurants, some shifts offer better earning opportunities than others. In most restaurants, dinners are more lucrative than lunches. This is because dinner menu prices are likely to be higher, guests are more likely to order drinks, and guests also are more likely to order fancier items, multiple courses, and side dishes. Friday and Saturday nights are likely to be the best nights since they typically have more customers and those customers are more likely to be letting loose and consequently spending more. Monday night is likely to be the worst night, with each successive weekday night being better.

Not all restaurants follow this pattern, however. In a business district, for example, lunches may offer better opportunities than dinners, and there may be no weekend service at all. Bear in mind, however, that a lunch-driven restaurant is still likely to follow part of the pattern—Monday is likely to be the slowest day, with each successive day offering greater earning opportunities.

To whatever extent you can, try to work a variety of shifts to learn which will be the most profitable for you. You might find that you can develop a group of regulars on a shift that other servers don't value. If so, you will be able to position yourself with management and fellow servers as being a good soldier in not just seeking the shifts that are obviously the well-paying ones.

Getting the Best Shifts

Knowing which shifts are potentially the most lucrative is only half of the battle, of course: you need to get these shifts. In many restaurants, shifts are assigned on the basis of seniority. However, in most restaurants, the best performing waiters—judged in terms of service, attitude, and reliability—will eventually be able to upgrade to the best shifts.

To get the best shifts management must be convinced that you deserve them and are capable of handling them. Convincing other servers of this will also ease your progress because they are less likely to object to management giving you good shifts if they know you are a fully capable server.

As a new server, picking up shifts from other servers is an excellent way to prove both that you are ready to work and able to manage a tougher section. If you pick up some closing shifts, for instance, you can show yourself capable of being a closing server and end up being given closing shifts on a permanent basis.

Once management considers you capable of handling the best shifts, the next step is to convince your managers that you deserve them. You can win favor with managers by:

- Being available to help out at any time, including filling in on shifts when someone else fails to show.

- Being happy and pleasant to deal with at all times.

- Becoming friends with the owner or manager.

THE MOST DESIRABLE POSITION WITHIN A SHIFT

Closing waiter. In most restaurants, being a closing server is a highly desirable position, because the manager typically reduces the number of servers until few remain during lunch and dinner service. If you are a very capable server, you may have the whole restaurant to yourself, which means more tables, more money, and of course more work. On the other hand, if you are the first "cut" (the first sent home), you will usually stay on through all the busy times and go home when things slow down, so your earnings per hour may be high, but your shifts short. Thus, being the first or second one cut can be good for students who have less time to work and need time for their studies.

Opening waiter. Opening servers are typically the weakest servers in restaurants. This is because there are likely to be relatively few diners during the opening hour or so, which means that even a less-capable waiter can manage the shift.

Bear in mind, however, that restaurant procedures vary, so the most desirable position depends on which position is given control of the most tables for the longest time. Note, too, that most servers are given the least demanding and least risky positions until they have proved that they can handle more.

Fighting For Shifts

Sometimes a restaurant will have more servers than it needs, which generally leads to many servers getting fewer shifts than they were accustomed to and several of them pressing management with requests for more hours all at the same time. In an effort to accommodate these requests, managers may suggest to non-complaining servers that they drop some of their shifts. In order to keep your shifts, you will need to be strong-willed and not give in to suggestion. In a corporate restaurant setting, by the way, managers can get into trouble for removing shifts from a server's schedule without his or her consent.

Getting the Best Station

Restaurants are usually divided into sections, with one waiter assigned to each. The tables in each section are close together to minimize the amount of walking the waiter has to do, and make it easier for the waiter to see what each table in his section requires.

Some sections are better to work than others are. For instance, a station close to the kitchen (to minimize the walk from the kitchen to the tables) yet not too close (because favored customers prefer not to be seated near the kitchen's noise and bustle) is considered prime territory. Expensive restaurants often have "power tables"—tables that are strategically located in the restaurants to give customers a full view of the room but without compromising their privacy. These are usually reserved for the restaurant's best customers, which makes them particularly desirable for servers.

Some restaurants change station assignments regularly; others assign on the basis of seniority. In many restaurants, the most senior or best waiters are given the largest or most desirable stations because they are able to handle more guests effectively or provide the best service. As in the case of getting the best shifts, the combination of demonstrating competence and gaining favor with management is likely to aid you in landing the best station.

MANAGERS DISCUSS HOW THEY ASSIGN SHIFTS AND SECTIONS

ASSIGNING SHIFTS

"You get the best shifts through a combination of longevity and being a strong server—and a bit of luck."

Irish restaurant manager

"The best sellers—who sell appetizers, desserts, and bottles of wine—get the best shifts."

Corporate casual chain manager

"We allocate our top shifts to our top guns, who train the new people. They get their choice of shifts."

Upscale restaurant manager

"The best servers get the biggest tips, and those with the highest tips get the best shifts and sections."

Irish restaurant manager

"We're unionized, so shifts are given out on the basis of seniority."

Hotel restaurant manager

ASSIGNING SECTIONS

"We give our two busiest sections to our best servers."

Asian restaurant manager

"Our best servers get our biggest and best sections."

Irish restaurant manager

CREATING REGULAR CUSTOMERS

THE VALUE OF REGULAR CUSTOMERS

Regulars are customers who come back in part to see and be served by you—because they know that you will take good care of them. They will be relatively easy to serve, too, because they won't require lengthy explanations of the menu and because you'll know their usual orders and preferences. They are also likely to tip particularly well as a thank-you for the personalized service.

Regular customers will almost never be rude to you, making it more pleasant to serve them. In addition, you are likely to develop a relationship with them (and should try to do so), so you'll exchange information with them as you would with friends—making the experience more pleasant for both of you. In addition, as you get to know their tastes, you'll help them discover new menu items they'll enjoy.

The benefits of cultivating regular guests is therefore obvious. But in some restaurants there will be little reason to expend the effort. For example, if your tourist-town restaurant serves people who are passing through for a few hours and are unlikely to return, you would be better off focusing on other ways to increase your earnings.

THE BENEFITS OF HAVING REGULAR SHIFTS

It is extremely difficult to develop regular customers if you work random or rotating shifts. People become regular customers of yours only if they know they can count on you being on duty at particular times each week.

Serving Regular Customers

Taking care of your regular customers can mean foregoing quick profits. For example, never push the day's "specials" if you know there really is nothing special about them or that they are special only because the restaurant has, for example, too much lamb with an expiration date of tomorrow. Regulars trust you to take good care of them, which certainly includes steering them away from questionable food.

Learn as much as you can about your guests without being intrusive. When you are waiting for some guests to finish their conversation before interrupting them to ask whether they'd like another drink before dinner, pay attention to what they're saying.

When a regular comes to your restaurant with friends, she will be particularly appreciative of your remembering her usual order. "Hello Ms. Gupta, it's wonderful to see you again. Shall I start you off with some papadoms and the chutney tray, followed by our mulligatawny soup, and then a chicken biryani and tarka dal?" This performance will demonstrate to her friends that she merits professional and helpful service.

Customers, especially regulars, like to feel wanted and appreciated. Here are some ways to show them they are appreciated:

- Try to have private tastings for regulars, if your manager permits, whether of food or wine. Or ask them to come in to sample some free appetizers.

- Know what you can offer for free without having to check with your manager.

- If you have a customer who is important to you, see whether you can have the chef come out to discuss a special dish, or what is particularly fresh and wonderful at the moment. Engage your regulars by asking the chef (whom you have, with any luck, befriended by now) to come out of the kitchen and ask your regular how he likes a particular dish prepared.

- If a regular customer has a standard order, such as having a Jameson on the rocks before dinner, order it for him as soon as you see him enter the restaurant. In all likelihood he will be delighted to have his drink arrive at the table at the same time he does. And even if he had not intended to order it this evening, he will nonetheless take it with pleasure because he will want to encourage you to continue giving him such excellent, personalized service.

- Many older guests will have trouble reading the menu without good light. Try to seat them at a well-lit table. If you have a mini-flashlight or some inexpensive reading glasses you can offer them, all the better.

- Some guests hate loud music. Learn this and seat them accordingly.

- You may want to make it easy for regulars to have their usual orders ready when they arrive. Thus, you could give them your contact details so they can text you with their request, and you can put in their order.

- If you know that several of your regulars are single and might like to meet someone suitable for dating, consider introducing them.

- Tell guests about any special events the restaurant will be holding. For example, if restaurant week is about to take place, by all means mention this.

LEARNING AND REMEMBERING GUESTS' NAMES

It's much easier to develop a regular customer if you know her name. Encourage the hostess to mention a guest's name whenever she is passing him to you. If a guest pays by credit card, always note her name and use it. Thanking her by name will please her since most of us feel our name is the greatest word in the language. Always use her last name rather than her first name, unless and until she suggests you call her by her first.

Once you learn a guest's name, use it several times in conversation with him or her. This will help you remember her name for the next hour or so, but not forever. Given that you will be learning dozens of names, you'll need a method to remember them for the next time these guests visit. Anytime you have a break, write down the names of the people you've just met, along with any relevant details:

- When she came in

- Which table she sat at, and in which seat

- A brief description of her

- How she was dressed

- What she carried

- What she ordered

- Any comments she made about the food

- Anything she shared about her evening (e.g., having just shopped for shoes) or life

It may be difficult to write this much in a brief break, especially if you need to cover several new guests. You may find it easier to speak into a digital tape recorder or your phone and then transcribe your notes after your shift is over or things have slowed down.

Keep a record on your primary computer or electronic device. Review your notes periodically so that you will be ready for any of the dozens of people in your records to make a second appearance. It will be helpful if you can access your records quickly in case someone familiar-looking walks in. Similarly, if someone has reserved a table in your section, you will want to be able to check on his name before he shows up.

The more you remember about someone, the more impressed she will be. If you remember that the last time she came in she had to return to pick up the shopping bag she had left, she will be very impressed. So, too, if you recall that she really liked the salmon special last month.

THE VALUE OF CUSTOMERS KNOWING YOUR NAME

If a customer knows your name:

- She may well ask to have you as her waiter the next time she comes to the restaurant. This is, of course, the way for her to become a regular customer of yours.

- She can recommend that her friends ask for you to be their waiter.

- If she likes your service, and the overall experience she had at the restaurant, she may provide a review on Yelp or elsewhere that includes your name. Employers tend to keep close track of such reviews and will sometimes reward you for positive mentions.

MANAGERS' AND SERVERS' ADVICE

REGARDING REGULAR CUSTOMERS

"The best servers get to know their guests and their guests ask for them."

Corporate casual restaurant manager

"Customers expect a good job. If you do a great job, they'll ask for you when they come back."

Fine dining restaurant owner

"Relate to customers on a personal level. Doing so leads to a real conversation."

Pub restaurant server

"If you can tell that someone is hosting an important business dinner, make him or her look good in front of the others."

Steak house manager

Serving Foreign Guests

The first rule in serving foreign guests is to speak very clearly and slowly. Thus, "What would you like?" rather than "Waddayawant?" Use standard English, without slang, colloquialisms, or local expressions.

When addressing your guests, try to do so somewhat formally if possible. Thus, "sir" or "madam" rather than "guys" or "folks" or "yunzguys" (with apologies to Pittsburgh).

Do not assume that someone struggling to express herself in English does not understand the language. She may well understand anything you say to or about her. By the same token, if you have a foreign guest, silence may not mean acceptance or a lack of questions. Instead, it may mean she is puzzled.

Culture

Try to be flexible and follow the lead of your guests. Be accommodating if they want something done that is contrary to American norms, such as serving the salad after the meal rather than before or with it.

Learn the needs and desires of your most frequent foreign guests. For instance:

- If you are serving Arabs, never use your left hand for service. The left hand is reserved for toilet matters.

- Many cultures do not emphasize speedy meals, so leaving the bill as soon as a table has finished ordering may be considered rude.

- Offer bottled water if possible. In many countries, this is the norm.

Foreign guests are especially likely to need and value help navigating the menu. Many will appreciate learning what the local specialties are, including whatever incorporates local products.

British Terminology

Many visitors are accustomed to British food terms. These guests include those from the British Commonwealth, such as Canadians, Kiwis, and Aussies, along with those who learned British English. A brief sampling of American terms and their British equivalents would include:

AMERICAN	BRITISH
Arugula	Rocket
Eggplant	Aubergine
French fries	Chips
Ham	Gammon
Hungry	Peckish
Napkin	Serviette
Okra	Lady fingers
Sausages	Bangers
Zucchini	Courgettes
Bordeaux red wine	Claret
German white wine	Hock

It is not essential that you learn a lot of British menu terms, but it would be helpful to know what the Brits call the items your restaurant serves. Being able to use this vocabulary will strike your "British-speaking" guests as unusual and very welcoming. It will certainly mark you as a professional trying to help them.

In fact, the most important difference between British and American (and European) restaurant terminology may concern the names of courses:

AMERICAN	BRITISH	CONTINENTAL EUROPEAN
Appetizer	Starter	Entrée
Entrée	Main course	Principle dish/plate
Dessert	Pudding	Dessert

Note the confusion around the term "entrée." Given that it translates from French as "first" or "beginning," it's peculiar that Americans use it not to mean a starter or first course, but a main course. Another term of confusion is, of all things, a martini. Many Europeans will order a martini, by which they mean straight vermouth rather than a gin (or vodka) and vermouth cocktail.

Promoting Tips

Many foreign guests will not understand that the way American waiters make their money is through discretionary tips. In their home countries, waiters may be paid adequate salaries or benefit from a service charge built into the price of the food and drink. As a result, many foreigners, including the Brazilians, Chinese, and French, see no need to leave any tip at all, and many others expect to tip only 5—10%. In Japan, tipping a waiter is an insult, implying that he or she depends upon the diner's charity to live.

The trick to getting these foreign guests to tip you well is to educate them about the system in place in America without being overbearing and seeming to demand a tip. You might try a pitch like the following:

"As you may know, waiters in the U.S.—like me—are paid through 'tips' diners leave for them. The usual tip that Americans leave in this restaurant is 15—20% of the total bill, depending upon how good the service has been. So for a bill of $80, the usual tip would be between $12 and $16. Please understand, though, that you are not obligated to leave any tip at all. It is your choice."

You could also write up something like this, get it approved by your manager, and hand it to your foreign guests. Before handing it to a guest, you could ask whether he is familiar with the American style of tipping. If he says no, you can hand him your write-up.

SOCIAL SCIENCE
TIPS TO EARN MORE

Social scientists have recently started studying what waiters and others who serve the public can do to improve customer satisfaction. Daniel Pinker in his book, *To Sell is Human,* and Michael Lynn of Cornell's Hotel School, have brought together studies examining a large number of variables in serving techniques. All of the following produced an increase in tips:

Personalizing Yourself

- Introduce yourself by name. Make sure you are friendly and sincere. Inquire as to whether the party has dined at the restaurant before—if the host has not so indicated.

- Stand out as an individual. Making yourself stand out as an individual rather than remaining a faceless server can apparently improve your tips. One technique researchers tested was having a waitress wear a flower in her hair, but the same would apply to someone wearing anything else distinctive, whether it was a silly fish tie or interesting hat.

- Make yourself as attractive as possible. Attractive waitresses get larger tips than less attractive waitresses. Increasing your attractiveness, such as by wearing makeup and becoming clothing, can increase your tips. (It is not clear to what extent—if at all—men can increase their tips by increasing their attractiveness.)

Showing Appreciation

- Write "thank you" on the check. All sincere expressions are likely to be helpful.

- Giving a customer candy. Leaving a mint at the end of a meal is meant to provoke a need in her to reciprocate your generosity.

Connecting with the Customer

- Squat down next to the table. Adjusting your physical position in this way brings you closer to your guests and increases eye contact, thereby increasing rapport. Although an excellent suggestion for those working in casual dining restaurants, it's not appropriate in fine dining restaurants.

- Praise diners' menu choices. Giving a diner sincere praise for his choice of food or wine will make him feel good and, consequently, feel good about you. Note the limits of this technique: telling a dozen diners at a table that they all made great choices, or that they chose the dozen entrées you most prefer, will ring hollow and the diners will treat your comments as silly and patronizing. On the other hand, if a guest chooses a bottle of wine that you know will match perfectly with the shellfish appetizer and fish main course he's ordered, noting in what way the match will be wonderful will strike the right chord with him.

- Repeat an order word for word. Politely mimicking a diner by repeating her order word for word suggests that you paid close attention to her and that you are treating her order with great care. Similarly, matching a customer's behavioral patterns (pace, vocabulary, volume of speech, facial expressions for example) also helps you to connect with her.

- Address customers by name. This demonstrates that they are recognized and important. And as has been recognized since time immemorial, the sweetest sound in any language is a person's own name.

Setting a Happy Tone

- Smile. Smiling makes you seem attractive, competent, and sincere. It also suggests you are friendly, happy to see the guests and to serve them, and easily approachable. It is one of the easiest but most important things you can do to set the right tone for your relationship with guests. And, after all, diners tip friendly waiters more than unfriendly waiters.

- Drawing a "happy face" on the check. Interestingly, the studies show that this increased tips for female servers but not for waiters, possibly because a smiley face is considered feminine.

- Forecasting good weather or drawing a picture of the sun on the check. Diners in a good mood leave bigger tips than diners in a sour mood. Forecasting that the weather is meant to be sunny and warm this weekend, or simply drawing a shining sun on a check, can help put diners in a cheerful mood.

There are other techniques that are worth trying, too:

- Nodding your head when you suggest a menu item may subtly help sell it.

- If a particular sports team matters greatly in your area (or just to the guests you have been serving), consider putting "Go Lions!" or "Go Devil Dogs!" on checks.

- Tell guests you are working to support your work as an actor, a serious jazz or classical musician, or even better, that you are working to pay for college. This strikes an upbeat note, whereas mentioning that you're working as a single mom to pay for your kid strikes a somber one.

SIMPLIFYING YOUR GUESTS' DECISIONS

Speeding your guests' decision-making may or may not increase the percentage they tip you, but it can reduce your workload and also help you turn tables. The technique for achieving this is to focus them on relatively few choices. In one famous experiment, researchers found that customers offered 24 varieties of jam bought only 10 percent as much jam as those offered just 6 varieties of jam. This insight is particularly useful when customers confront a multi-page menu for the first time. Thus, asking which of 25 draft beers a guest would like, try to narrow down their choices. "Would you like a local craft brew? We have two from breweries right here in town, and one from the coast." Similarly, when guests are completely undecided about meal choices, try mentioning the two or three specials on offer.

DETERMINING WHAT WORKS FOR YOU

Although these techniques have been found to work for people in a variety of circumstances, this is no guarantee that they will work for you. After all, your personality and personal style, combined with the environment you work in, may result in some of these techniques working well for you and others not working at all. We suggest you try the ones that strike you as most appropriate for your circumstances and your customers.

It can be hard to tell, however, whether one or another technique is actually working for you. If you try a dozen different techniques with one table, you won't know whether the good tip was because these diners always tip well, were in a good mood before they came in, or one or another—or a bunch—of the techniques paid off. The way to test these techniques is to try using one technique at a time, randomizing when you do and don't use it, and recording the results. Let's say you decide to try the "forecasting good weather" technique. You can "randomize" the effort by alternating between using it and not using it. If you use it with your first table, don't use it with your second table, use it with the third, don't use it with the fourth, and so on, you should begin to see a pattern in the results. And if you keep track of the tip percentages you get from the tables that do and the tables that do not receive that treatment, after 80 to 100 checks you should have a good set of data to judge whether that particular technique is successful.

To make this easier, consider having a colleague do the same with his tables. Compare notes after each of you has handled 50 tables or so. If you and your colleague each work twenty shifts a month, with approximately a dozen checks per shift, you should be able to test about five techniques in a month.

Maximizing Your Income

Chapter Nine

Thinking Of Your Shift and Station As a Business— Your Business

As you progressively apply and master the tools and ideas we've given you in the rest of the book, you might opt to take another large step toward earning a lot of money. This involves treating your shift and station as your own business.

How would this work? How can you run your own business while still working at your restaurant? As a server, you have been granted an opportunity to make money from someone else's location, which happens to be furnished and stocked with a complete inventory of products. Your commission is 15—20% (or more) of what you sell— without your having to take any business risk by leasing space or purchasing inventory in the hope you will eventually be able to sell it.

If you start to think creatively about making the most of this opportunity, both you and your restaurant stand to gain a great deal of money. So instead of thinking that you work for a restaurant, think about how the restaurant is set up to help you run your own mini-business.

Developing Customers

Once you consider yourself to be running a business, you may cease to rely on the restaurant to provide you with all of your customers. Yes, the restaurant may provide you with a steady flow of customers for an hour or two on most nights, but think about how much more you would make if you had a steady flow throughout each shift.

Now that this is your business, start marketing it. As you begin your own promotional campaign, you can use the restaurant's cards and write your information on the back of them. The next step is to get business cards made. They should include your name; the name, location, and contact details of your restaurant; the hours or shifts you work; and the times when you can provide a VIP service. Considering how inexpensive business cards are these days—500 for about $10—it's well worth the effort.

Networking in your Neighborhood

Hand out your business cards to all the people you regularly encounter or do business with, including your dry cleaner, hairdresser or barber, bank tellers, and so on. Even if you don't have dozens of people in your orbit that you can approach, there are still the businesses near the restaurant for you to reach out to. Each local business will have multiple people if not dozens or hundreds working in or connected with it. A good way to do this is to thank them for taking such good care of you and then ask if you could return the favor by giving them some special treatment at your restaurant.

You can refine your efforts by targeting those most likely to appreciate your kind of restaurant. If yours is a very high end restaurant, target local businesses that cater to a fancy clientele. This could be an expensive flower shop or custom tailor. If your establishment features organic ingredients, target health food stores and the like.

YOUR MARKETING PITCH

Tell people about your restaurant, then note the times when you can provide them with a really special service. These will be your slow times, such as before the dinner rush. For instance, you may get busy at 7:30 pm, but have an almost empty section from 6:00 pm until 7:30 pm. Any guests you can get to start their meals at 6:00 or 6:30 will be "found money" for you. You will certainly have the time to provide extra special care during this slow time.

Also consider giving a personal card to customers suggesting they text or call you on your cell phone if they had less than a fabulous experience.

PROVIDING VIP SERVICE

You may need to get your manager's approval for the actions suggested here. And you obviously should have established some credibility with her before approaching her.

Explain how your marketing efforts can be a win-win situation for both you and the restaurant. For example, if you have people coming in during your establishment's slow periods, you are not only increasing your own profits, but also those of the restaurant. Once your manager understands this, she may permit you to seat your guests at the best table (such as a chef's table), give them a free appetizer or glass of wine, introduce them to the chef or owner, give them a tour of the kitchen, or do something else that makes them feel special.

Consider what 3—5 things you could do (and your manager will let you do) to make celebrating guests feel special for each of the following occasions:

- Child's birthday
- Adult's birthday
- Work success
- Wedding anniversary
- High school or college graduation
- Whatever else guests celebrate at your restaurant

It's fairly easy to make someone feel special without going to great lengths. For example, if it's someone's anniversary, you can have the restaurant owner stop by the table and then introduce everyone. "Ms. Simpson, have you met our lucky couple? Mr. and Mrs. Martinelli are celebrating fifty years of marriage tonight. Isn't that wonderful?"

REFERRAL CUSTOMERS

Referral customers, like regular customers, tend to be a pleasure to wait on. They want to reflect well on the person who referred them and with whom they probably do substantial business or with whom they have substantial social contact. They know they will get special treatment, even if they haven't done anything to deserve it. As a result, they are likely to be in a good mood and not terribly finicky. Your approach: "Ah, Mary sent you, eh? That's great. That means I can offer you a free appetizer. In addition, there are a couple of specials that don't appear on the menu that I can offer you."

You will also be able to form a relationship with a referral customer. You have the opportunity right from the beginning to ask her questions about how she knows Mary, whether she works in the area, what sort of work she does, where she lives, where else she likes to dine, and so on. As a result of this connection and the special service you are providing, you should be able to convert many referral customers into regular customers.

Make sure the hostess knows that you are the one who provides special treatment for different occasions, so that she seats in your section anyone who has announced such an occasion to her.

LEVERAGING SOCIAL MEDIA

Social media is obviously an increasingly powerful marketing tool. Have people praise you on review sites such as Yelp. When they rate the restaurant, have them note that your service was excellent and the reason they'll be coming back. If your friends visit the restaurant, consider having them leave this sort of review—without making it obvious that they are your pals, or course.

Any sort of celebration is worthy of a picture. And whatever your guests post to their networks will be better advertising for you than anything you put up yourself. Just be sure to have them tag you or your restaurant in their photos.

Grab any reason to take a picture for your guests. For example, you may overhear them saying that this is their first get-together since college—or maybe it's a relief to have an evening without working late for the first time this month. Even insubstantial events can be reason enough to take a picture for them. These pictures are likely to be broadcast to friends and others. Again, ask them to tag you or your establishment.

> **A FINE DINING RESTAURANT OWNER'S EXHORTATION**
>
> Look at it like you're leasing this space for the night and you can make as much as you can sell. Make the most of it.

ACKNOWLEDGMENTS

We have interviewed hundreds of people in the process of writing this book. Not all of them wanted to be given credit—some out of a desire for anonymity, others because that would require jumping through public relations and legal department hoops—but we are delighted to list below those who were willing to be acknowledged. Most of them are managers or owners of restaurants, but a substantial number were servers (and many who are now managers and owners started in the industry as servers). We also spoke with numerous bussers and hosts as well as various human resource and operations directors and vice presidents, trainers of restaurant personnel, banquet captains, bartenders and bar managers, chefs and executive chefs, and even a few restaurant lawyers and investors.

The restaurants and other eating establishments at which they work cover a wide range:

- More than thirty states, from Massachusetts to Hawaii, and Minnesota to Texas—as well as overseas

- Center city, suburban, and town locations

- Just-opened as well as long-established

- In multiple categories, from every day to fancy: whether hotel, airport, corporate casual or corporate upscale, neighborhood, fine dining or even ultra high-end restaurants; or private clubs and bars, wineries, or caterers

We would like to thank the following people (credited by first name or first and last names, according to their desire, and listed alphabetically by restaurant or company) for all of their help and insights:

Al and Al's Stein Haus (Susan Patterson, owner, Sheboygan WI)

Alero (Vidal Garcia, manager, Washington DC)

Amaya (Jamilla Fernandes, manager, London UK)

Los Andes (Ali, manager, Providence RI)

Andrea's (Costa Roussis, manager, London UK)

Ankara (Oznur Basha and Cserhan Iskenderov, managers, Washington DC)

Applebee's (Alexis Attish, server, San Diego CA)

Babushka (Michael Carey, server and bartender, Walnut Creek CA)

Berkeley Hall Country Club (John Soulia, food and beverage director, Bluffington SC)

Bev's Wine Bar (Paul, co-owner, Minneapolis, MN)

B55 (Jonathan, manager, San Francisco, CA)

Biaggi's Ristorante Italiano (Kevin Read, vice president of operations, Deer Park, Naperville and elsewhere in IL)

Bistro du Coin (Ayça Kargin, manager, Washington DC)

Blackfinn (Alexa Stafford, manager, Washington DC)

The Black Sheep (Dave, manager, Philadelphia PA)

Bloomington Country Club (Amanda Mohan, banquet captain, Bloomington IL)

The Boat House (Malcolm Bailey, line cook, Vancouver BC)

Boisdale of Bishopsgate (Becky, server, London UK)

The Bombay Club (Daya Kotian, manager—and manager of Rasika, Washington DC)

Boodell and Domanski (Al Domanski, lawyer, Chicago IL)

Border Café (Eila Pereira, manager, Cambridge MA)

Bravo Brasserie (Tait, manager, Providence RI)

Bub City (Clay Tormey, manager, Rosemont IL)

Bubba Gump (Jon Pira, server, San Francisco CA)

Buca di Beppo (Duaa Albethiny, manager, Washington DC)

Cabo Cantina (Meghan, bartender, Santa Monica CA)

California Pizza Kitchen (Charles MacMahon, server, Walnut Creek CA)

Campino's (Marilene, server, East Providence RI)

Caña (Sally Mead, server and bartender, Oakland CA)

Candela Tapas Lounge, (Zoey, supervisor, Hanover NH)

The Capital Grille (Caity Arico, manager, Providence RI)

Captain D's (Wendy Harkness, chief people officer, Nashville TN)

Catch 15 (Fessaha, manager, Washington DC)

Cheeky Monkey (Barry, manager, Boston MA)

The Cheesecake Factory (Pete Recine, manager, Providence RI)

Chevy's (Brittany Lowell, server, Emeryville CA)

Chima (Vinicius Morais, manager, Philadelphia PA)

Chop Shop (Gunnar Poole, server and bartender, Chicago IL)

Claim Jumper (Suhail Rafidi, server, Concord CA)
Claim Jumper (Billy Corona, manager, Sacramento CA)
Clean Plate (Lauren, owner, and Kyra, server, Providence RI)
Clyde's (Joe Fasnelli, manager, Chevy Chase MD)
Le Colonial (Antonio, maitre d', Chicago IL)
Comptoir Libanais (Hatem, manager, London UK)
Le Coq D'Or (Fausto Lozano, server, Chicago IL)
Côte Brasserie (Georgina Ocsenas, manager, London UK)
Cutter's Bar & Grill (Charles K. Nolen, owner, Detroit MI)

Del Frisco's Double Eagle Steak House (Matthew de Binder, manager, Boston MA)
Del Frisco's Double Eagle Steak House (Elissa Pablo, general manager, Massachusetts)
Dev's on Bank (Emily, server and bartender, New London CT)
District Anchor (Tony Palmer, manager, Washington DC)

Eddie Merlot's (Geoff Stiles, president, Arizona and eight other states)
Eureka! (Kellie Bondelie and Christina Knoll, managers; Jesse Baughman, bartender and consultant; Sarah Foley, server and bartender; Brennan Patrick, server and key holder; and Amelia Williams and Matthew Hannon, servers, Berkeley CA)
Eureka! (Stephen Weber, manager and server, Boulder CO)

Fast Food Management Inc. (John Regis, owner, Puerto Rico)
Favorite Bistro (Jeremy, owner, and Leah, manager, Las Vegas, NV)
Fleming's Steakhouse (Floyd Crisp, operating partner, Providence RI)
Fogo da Chão Brazilian Steakhouse (Diego Christensen, manager, Philadelphia PA)
Fuji Mountain (Roger, manager, Philadelphia PA)

The Grain Store (Patricia Pereira, server, Gatwick Airport UK)
The Grill on the Alley (Courtney, server, Chicago IL)

Hackneys on Lake (Jim and Elaine Masterson, owners, Glenview IL)
Hard Rock Café (Marcus Hernandez, manager, San Francisco CA)
Harvest (Steve Pereira, manager, Cambridge MA)
Hearth Pizza Tavern (Rob Phillip, partner and chef, Sandy Springs GA)
Henrietta's Table (Sarah, manager, Cambridge MA)
High Tides (Abby, general manager, Providence RI)
HMR Acquisitions Company, Inc.—owner of multiple Hoosier-Mex restaurants (Cody, marketing and beverage manager, Indiana)

In N Out, (Brandon Klein, server, Sacramento CA)
Indian Cuisine (Islam Najrul, server, Philadelphia PA)

International House Catering (Greg Tilden-Cline, server, Berkeley CA
Istanbul-lu (Hussein, manager, Somerville MA)
The Ivy (Andrius Izgamaitis, manager, London UK)
Ivy at the Glen (Jimmy Lambatos, owner, Denver, CO)

Jade Tree (Shu Yan, owner, Providence RI)
Jim and Chelsea Catering (Jim, owner, Saratoga, NY)
JJ Thai (Roger, manager, Philadelphia PA)
Joe's Crab Shack (Larry Hutt, manager, Wilmington DE)

Kaffa Ethiopian Cuisine (Shahtia, owner, Berkeley CA)
Kim's Catering (Kim Vitko, owner, Cleveland OH)
Kleos (Lauren Lynch, owner—and owner of Rosalina, Providence RI)

La Forge Casino (JR, manager, Newport RI)
Lazy Dog (Sam, server, Concord CA)
Legal Seafood (Courtney Bolinger, manager, Cambridge MA)
Leverage Partners (Bart Perkins, IT consultant to major restaurant
    groups, Louisville KY)
Little Ethiopia (Aida Teklemariam, server, Los Angeles CA)

Madeira (Zita, manager, East Providence RI)
Main Sail (Davon Saunders, manager, Newport RI)
Marcus Hotels & Resorts (Barbara Gromacki, vice president of human
    resources, and Jan, training manager, Milwaukee WI)
Maui Brewing Co. (Justin, bartender, Waikiki HI)
McBride's (Brendan, manager, Providence RI)
McClellan's Bar and Restaurant (Satoko Okuma, manager, Washington DC)
McCormick and Schmick (Cory Spear, manager, Providence RI)
Mel's Lone Star Lanes (Tracy Waters, food and beverage manager,
    Georgetown TX)
Mok Ban (Ella, manager, Providence RI)
Molana (Nick, server, Watertown MA)
Moonlight Basin (Mike Wilcynski, general manager, Big Sky MT)
Moro Sushi (Ms Kim, owner, Newport RI)
Morton's Steakhouse (Ramon, server, San Francisco CA)
Mr. Cooper's (Mary Wilson, manager, Manchester UK)

North Gate Grill (William Bright, manager, Washington DC)

O'Faiolain's (Matt Keibel, general manager, Sterling VA)
Olive Garden (Jack Muller, server, food runner, busser, and Josh Muller,
    server, San Francisco CA)
Opa (Joyce Karam, manager, Providence RI)

Organic Greens (Suren, owner, Berkeley CA)
The Other Place Bar & Grill (Dan Fulda, general manager, Duluth MN)
Outback Steakhouse (Justin Park, busser and host, Pinole CA)

Padre (Summer Noviello and Daisy Wanger, servers, Long Beach CA)
Parkside (Adam, manager, Providence RI)
Patton Valley Vineyard (Monte Pitt, owner, Gaston OR)
PF Chang (James Fleming, server, Denver CO)
PF Chang (Isaac Reyes, manager, Providence RI)
Le Pho (Lee Hoffman, server, Berkeley CA)
Pig & Goose (Craig, server, London UK)
PJ Clarke's (Robin Jones, manager Robert Buggs, server, Washington DC)
Platano (Jose Diaz, server and shift lead, Berkeley CA)

The Red Lion (Ryann, server, Chicago IL)
The Red Parrot (Samantha Martel, manager, Newport RI)
The Restaurant at Meadowood (Liz Murray, server, Napa CA)
Rhine Haus (Kimber Pearce, server, Tacoma WA)
The Ritz Carlton (Justine, hostess and server, Chicago IL)
Robert's Restaurant (Camillo Rivera, manager, Washington DC)
Rosebud Steak House (Natalya Veehara, maître d', Chicago IL)
Ruby Tuesday (Latricia Adams, manager, Philadelphia PA)
Ruth's Chris Steak House (Jennifer Tronoski, manager, Philadelphia PA)

S & S (Chandra, manager, Cambridge MA)
Saturn Café (Danny Knoester, server, Berkeley CA)
Scarpetta (Ennio Ciminelli, manager, Philadelphia PA)
Scopo Di Vino (Tim, owner, San Francisco CA)
Shiraz (Paul, manager, Watertown MA)
Sidebar at Whiskey Row (Chip Hechert, managing partner, Louisville KY)
Smoke House (Luke Devine, manager—and manager of The Mooring, Newport RI)
Speisekammer (Robbie Hollis, busser, Alameda CA)
Spice Monkey (Nora Paholak, server and manager, Oakland CA)
Stonebridge Gold and Country Club (Kenneth Midlan, executive chef, Boca Raton FL)
Sura (Hannah, manager, Providence RI)
Suya African-Caribbean Grill (Sanjita, cashier, Berkeley CA)
Sweet Butter Restaurant and Catering (Emily Smith, owner, Sherman Oaks CA)
Sylvain (David Charlie Blessant, cook, New Orleans LA)

Talon Consulting (Sindie Read, educator, Reno NV)
Texas Spice (Alicia, manager, Dallas TX)
TGI Friday (Diana Poole, manager, Pittsburgh Airport PA)

Thai Chef (Scott Zheng, manager, Washington DC)

Thaikhun (Jake, supervisor, Oxford UK)

Tiki's Bar and Grill (Blake, server, Waikiki HI)

Tinto (Brett Meier-Tomkins, director of operations—also director of operations for Amado, Volvér, and other Chef Garces restaurants, Philadelphia PA and Atlantic City NJ)

Tir na Nog (John Doherty, manager, Philadelphia PA)

El Torito (Megan Cornelius, server, Sacramento CA)

Toscana (Dorian Kalaja, manager, New York NY)

Tria (Megan, manager, Philadelphia PA)

Tribu (Jose, server, Emeryville CA)

Trinity Brewhouse (Carolyn, server, Providence RI)

Triptych (Ben Alvers and Thomas Churchill, servers, San Francisco CA)

Vejigantes (Yajaira, server and bartender, Boston MA)

La Viña (Ines, manager, Manchester UK)

Wagamama (Dixon, manager, Boston MA)

The Wells (Eilish Farell, server, Hampstead UK)

Wollensky Grill (John, manager, New York NY)

The Wolseley (Diana, server, London UK)

Zazie (Jen Bennett Piallat, owner; Mario Rojas, general manager; Yonny Trujeque, server; and Richard Parham, server, San Francisco CA)

Zsavooz Grill and Garden (Nick and Tara Roberts, owners, Cedar Falls IA)

Made in the USA
Middletown, DE
25 March 2022